Kornel Makuszynski

Arabian Affairs

Translated by Sebastian Paluch

ZALTE
PUBLISHING

Published by Zalte Publishing
PO BOX 3282 Swindon SN2 9DZ
www.zalte.com

First published in Polish as Awantury Arabskie in 1913
This translation published by Zalte Publishing 2007
Text copyright © Kornel Makuszynski, 1913
Translation copyright © Sebastian Paluch, 2007
All rights reserved

The moral right of the author and translator has been asserted

This book is subject to the condition that it shall not be resold,
lent, hired out or otherwise circulated without the express prior consent
of the publisher.

Edited by Ruth Blaikie of FirstEditing.com

Layout by Robert Lis
Cover design by Frontdesign.pl

ISBN 9-780955-662805

Contents

The Eighth Voyage of Sindbad the Seaman

On the next day, friends gathered again at home of rich Sindbad (they and this muleteer that envied him his treasures), wondering immensely why he invited them for a feast for the eighth time, having told them all about his miraculous voyages already. Their faces drew, for they mused deeply, sighing from time to time, which greatly retains nimbleness of mind, reinvigorating it with fresh air.

That's how the illustrious seaman, Sindbad, most famous of all the seamen, not only in Baghdad, but in all the lands inhabited by the faithful, found them. He greeted them earnestly with a bow, then having stroked his fragrant beard, spake thus:

"One could think, my friends, looking at your faces at the moment that you are of nature thick, like mangy mules, which can be easily bought near Hassan's house; but I know that it is only amazement appearing on your faces and that you shall brighten your frowned foreheads, having learned, what the reason was, for inviting you for a feast for the eight time, although mutton got dearer, and a basket of dates costs perhaps more than all the emeralds in the Caliph's treasury. Be seated then and enjoy your meal, as much as you can stand, and even more than you can stand, so that no one said that seaman Sindbad, having acquired great riches, stinted his friends mutton and abundance of garlic. I shall tell you then, trying not to bore you too much, my noble friends and the Prophet's favourites, what the matter is.

This said, he clapped his hands, and the slaves, as if emerging out of thin air, started to bring in steaming food on golden and silver dishes. Their nostrils began to tremble, for each of them—having spent his day on labourious swindle: one weighing spices, on scales resembling paralytic man, the other cutting fabrics, so delicate that it shrunk in his hands and there was always less of it than needed—wanted now to sustain his body, which the Prophet forbade not, even recommended, if only one didn't have to pay for it.

So they got to work with solemnity, not hurrying too much, deeply convinced that even a wildest ram while alive, would not escape from the dish, even less so, being quartered to pieces with able hand of the Black cook, whom may Allah give long years, and few children stealing raisins and garlic from under his hand.

So one of them after another would plough through the huge chunks and ravished with the smell of the meat, flavoured with seventy-seven spices, would squint his eyes slightly, as if seeing heavens door, wide open; and the other, sitting next to him and waiting his turn, would open his eyes widely and mutter anxiously, suitable verse of Quran, in which between the others one could hear following blessings: "His hand will droop, so much takes this thief, his belly bigger than brains. Would that you choke on it, you unclean dog, uncle of a camel and brother of a jackal! How come the Prophet doesn't smack him on the mug, seeing what this son of Ali Baba is doing."

And when his turn came, he would smile blissfully, and the next one would wish him with all his heart, all the diseases that could be found in Baghdad, leprosy most of all, for it lasts long and one cannot get accustomed to it easily.

They would then eat in silence and ably tasting, and learned from the excellent sheep taste that everything is right with the world and that the blessing is upon it. How could otherwise the beast so foolish as a sheep carry so much fat on it? Many hours passed them thus, until Sindbad's friends felt that they were full, so having licked their fingers, not to stain their clothes, they started to dip their hands in silver bowls full of scented water, which at this moment lost much of its fragrance and became thick like waters of this sea, which they call Dead.

And when the slaves, turning their heads away and holding silver bowls with this water as far as they could, disappeared, motioned Sindbad the seaman that his friend be all ears; so they sat in circle and digesting sweetly, listened, what he was about to reveal. And he spoke:

"You visited me seven times, and I have told you about my seven voyages that are written down on donkeyskin in the Caliph's library, in One Thousand and One Nights collection. I have told you all that was, and all that was not, for Allah didn't give speech to his servants so that they told the truth. For he shall always recognize it, and cannot be bothered with anything else."

"You said, Sindbad!" answered to this rich dyer from the neighbourhood of the Eastern Gate. And Sindbad continued:

"I shall not reproach you for these two handfuls of dates and delicacies, which you put in your bosom, thinking that no one was watching, I will only tell you that whomever that having eaten to the full, wishes to interrupt me, I will have enumerated hundred lashes, so that his heels will resemble buttocks of a donkey, that has been beaten for twenty years."

"Shut your gob, worthy Yusuf!" told him politely the other, who suddenly desired some sleep. And Sindbad carried on:

"You know how I travelled to diamond valley and how I was carried off in Roc's talons, what splendid deeds I accomplished, famed throughout the world, what scary journeys I made, over which I acquired my fortune. But I have not told you everything. You know nothing about my scariest journey, during which I suffered a lot and brought back most precious treasure that Allah can give a man—a faithful wife; for I possess a wife who has never betrayed me and never will, which I can bear witness to and swear on Prophet's beard!

Here though, he ceased talking, for the blessed smile adorned his rugged face; Sindbad melted into ecstasy, and having lifted his head up like an old goat, looked in the ceiling, so he could not see his friends elbow each other, grin craftily and whisper: "Blasphemes this man and dares to lie too much!" Soon they ceased talking too though, for the fearless seaman began climbing down slowly the Jacob's ladder of delights, and having noticed that he sat on bent legs, just like the others, continued:

"Thinking that I had accomplished a lot, perhaps more than many that swagger and demand honours, I decided to rest and enjoy my riches sensibly and worthily. My soul though, adventure hungry and restless like an Anatolian mare, suddenly stung by a gad-fly in a tender spot, wallowed with me on my bed and not letting me sleep, would say: 'Why do you grow listless Sindbad, why do you put on weight in idleness, O fearless seaman? Have you travelled the entire world, have you seen everything that lives for glory of Allah? You have faced death seven times already, why shouldn't you face it for the eighth time, already accustomed to its sight?'

"This is what my soul was telling me, and I was hesitating for a long time, for I was afraid that at the moment of my departure, the beautiful Fatma, the baker's daughter, on account of me, being six months pregnant, would raise a yell throughout Baghdad, which wouldn't please me, for this virgin is capable of screaming so loudly that the dromedaries startle. So I called her to me and offered her a hundred coins and seven goats, which she willingly accepted, and I realized that I acted amiss, for when she was leaving, she told me that my gift came as a nice surprise, for she had been sure that not me, but certain ginger scribe of Vizier was father of her baby, or maybe cobbler Ibrahim. She also had some suspicions about two whirling dervishes. But she had never even thought of me.

"Very angry and full of disappointment, I ordered to prepare everything that was needed on a journey that can last a year or even ten. I loaded the ship with scented wood, saffron and fabrics and set sail West, which made no difference anyway, for I had to shipwreck somewhere, to have adventures, which can be easily understood by anyone who read One Thousand and One Nights.

"And so we sailed for twenty days and twenty nights, entertaining ourselves with singing and a not very crooked dice game, when I began to recognize various islands where I had experienced horrid mortifications; at this sight my heart swooned and I wanted to come back, when suddenly the storm broke and carried us from this place for fifty-three days and equal number of nights, wanting to scare us, but we stood strong, despite being exceedingly seasick due to the tempest. And one night, when the troubled sleep overpowered us, we felt with horror that something was going wrong with the ship. 'Here we go again!' I thought and having taken to the deck, in my underwear only, I felt hair raising on my head, for the ship, rushed with some immense traction, although the wind ceased blowing, was rushing with the speed of a startled mule towards the rugged rocks; I turned back quickly then and started to run down the deck in direction opposite to the ship's motion, so when its bow hit the rocks with great peal and smashed to pieces on the spot, I jumped off its stern into the sea, without even harming a hair on my head."

Interrupted there Sindbad and looked around on faces of his friends, who were all asleep, but they woke up immediately when silence fell, and started to talk quickly: "Yes, this is strange!" or "Allah is the greatest!" or "O, you suffered a lot!"

But the illustrious seaman stroked his beard and said:

"This is the mere beginning of my new torment, scariest of the all I have been through before."

So they stopped falling asleep and listened carefully, not reproaching themselves, for failing to hear the introduction, for all the introductions to all the Sindbad's voyages were always the same. Spoke seaman Sindbad:

"In my eyes the ship disappeared in the abyss and the sea closed over it, entombing my sandalwood, my saffron, and fifty sailors. I became terrified, but the terror invigorated me, so I started to swim towards the coast; I had just managed to grasp the rock with my hand, but immediately, having screamed, I slipped back into the sea, my hand severely burnt, for the rock was as hot as red-hot iron. Swimming, I started to weep bitterly, as I had done many times before, for I realized that fate wanted to put me to the test again, as if it couldn't have done the same, to a better effect, with someone else.

"I grizzled at my misfortune so loudly that the shoal of dolphins gathered around me and swimming right next to me, were showing me their compassion; so when I weakened, I sat on the back of the biggest dolphin that carried me willingly and with visible joy, and although it was not pleasant for me, for I had to submerge whenever he pleased, but still I thanked heavens for help in my immense misery. This is how I was swimming around for twenty-seven days suffering hunger and thirst and became so gaunt that I was almost translucent. On the twenty-eighth day only, I managed to land on this fearful shore that filled me with a strange suspicion that I would meet my death here or something even worse.

"I lied as if dead and tried to eat salty seashore sand, when suddenly I saw with horror, jumping around me on the sand, human heads, very handsome, staring at me with inquisitive eyes. I rose, overtaken with horrible fear, and perceived people standing in the distance, all of them headless.

"I found out later that dwellers of this land can easily detach their heads from the neck and send it for a quick scout around, if they do not wish to expose themselves to danger.

"I could not believe my eyes and wondered greatly at this magnificent implementation, when suddenly all the heads came running to their masters, and they—having tidied up soiled with sand hair, or having wiped with the sleeve a hairless skull, had some of them been bald—replaced the heads skilfully on their necks and all headed for me.

"I trembled out of fear, but thinking to myself that I had seen even greater wonders before, I waited, what they had to say; and they, coming closer, marvelled much and having noticed that I ate sand, they brought round a white goat and made me suck its udder, which not only reminded me infancy times, but also reinvigorated me greatly.

'We are the servants of King Babu, one of them told me later, come with us!'

"But since I forgot art of walking, they heaved me on their shoulders and carried me in triumph, wondering how light I was. When I was put down on my legs again, I noticed I was in a palace so enormous, as I had never seen before, although I had seen all the Caliph's palaces. It was palace of King Babu, reigning the vast nation, capable of tossing their heads like a stone; he himself was seated on a throne, embedded with more pearls than there is ulcers on leper's body, and was so sad that despite the shining sun, there was dusk around him and as if fog; he was a handsome man and very portly, but his soul must have been tormented with sorrow, for he beheld me with gruesome sight and said:

'Tell me, what is your death of choice?'

"I wondered at this question, for I was innocent, and didn't deserve death. Therefore I answered:

'I want, O Mightiest King, to live ten years shorter than you, whom I wish six thousand years of life!'

Then he wondered in turn.

'Don't you know, foreigner,' he said, his voice sad, 'that I died long ago?'

'I don't know about that, O Grandest Sultan!' was my answer, 'but if things be so, then have yourself wrapped in a shroud and buried in the ground.'

"King Babu ruminated upon my answer and pondered my words for ten days and ten nights, then he summoned me and said:

'Repeat once again what you have said, for I have forgotten, what exactly your words were!'

"I repeated them, and he, having withdrawn to his chambers, mused upon it for twenty days and twenty nights, and then having come out to see me, he said kindly:

'You rightly said!'

"Then he asked where I had come from and what fate had chased me into this country, so I recounted to him ornately and eloquently, what unparalleled sufferings had befallen me on my journey and how much I longed to return to my homeland. He enjoyed my tongue, for he summoned the Grand Vizier and all the ministers, and had them give me magnificent clothes and take care of me. And I, touched with this evidence of excellent favours, dropped to his feet, calling out:

'O mightiest ruler! Even today I would set sails for my homeland, but I swear you that I am not moving from here, until I discover what the reason of your sorrow is, and before I find cure for this sorrow. I would rather my gums decayed and eyes flown out, than behold your suffering; so tell me then, my king, what worries you?'

"King Babu mused long, whether he could reveal secrets of his heart to a foreign stranger. Finally though, despite the noble density of his mind, he understood that had he not, I would end up with no adventure to tell and this tale should end with nothing. Therefore he said:

'Realize then, wise foreigner that I had seven-hundred wives.'

'Allah Rossoulah!'' I shouted in surprise.

'And all seven-hundred of them betrayed me,' finished the king and wept so bitterly that my heart bled.

'So how can I be happy, being unable to find a woman, who loving me would persevere in it until death?'

'What do I care about treasures and lands, innumerable herds of camels, elephants, donkeys and goats, when I possess not even one woman? I am not even demanding her for me any more, for sorrow weakened my manly powers, but I shan't laugh before I find out that in my country, there is at least one woman who can be faithful. Why aren't you crying with me, Sindbad?'

'Your Majesty!' I answered, 'It cannot be! And although etiquette dictates that I cry when your noble eyes weep, I am not doing it, because I am busy thinking. Listen to me, O Wise King Babu! Here, I want to rejoice your elevated heart and find a faithful woman in your state.'

"King Babu reeled of amazement on his throne, and I carried on:

'I shall find a woman and marry her, and then we shall do a trial with her, and should she betray me, do with me, my lord, whatever you pleased; but should she resist the temptation and remain faithful to me, you shall give her to me as a property, and with her a ship, for me to come back to my homeland. Let me marry at least thrice though, for considering you have been betrayed by seven-hundred wives, what can I do, having only three?!'

'Good! answered King Babu, 'I swear on both my old and new sceptre, for I have two, that if you succeed, you will rejoice me, and I will make you rich and happy; but should your three wives betray you, I will have a camel's harness made of your skin, your eyes thrown to the crows, and your heart grilled on a slow fire.'

"Sudden cold embraced me, although the heat was unbearable, and only then had I realized what I dared; I was only counting on a lucky coincidence, knowing that had Allah remained single that was only because he knew women well. So I left, trembling with all my body, and started to ruminate in solitude upon what I should do, to ensure the fidelity of a woman: should I marry a young woman, she would betray me because she is young; and should I marry old and washy witch, she would betray me even easier, wanting to pretend to be young, and everybody knows that seitan stokes up an old oven.

"Desperation befell me, and I would have escaped from this dreadful country, had not the Prophet spirited me at the last minute. So I embarked on the search for a wife, having taken the grand reti-nue with me, one-hundred camels in excellent harnesses, one-thou-sand slaves, and fifty chests of clothes alone. I had my hair curled and cleaned of vermin each day, and so I roamed the country, searching diligently. Seeing the grand foreigner, everybody dropped to my feet, and women, even the married ones, were sending their slaves, asking me to repose under their roof, which was filling me with great worry.

"One day I noticed marvellous phenomenon: on a white donkey there rode a petite figure, enwrapped in a gold interweaved cloak. I could see that the eyes, looking from under the charshaf, were mod-est and of surprising beauty and something struck me to follow her. I found out she was a daughter of a rich prince, who having realized I was King Babu's favourite, agreed to bestow her hand upon me.

"I brought her to the king's palace and confessed her infinite love, and she, to my immense joy, swore that she had never seen a man more handsome than me and vowed to love me forever. I surrounded her with luxury and from sunrise to sunset, lying at her feet, I was weeping with joy and caressed her with most beautiful words, and she would listen with graceful heart and swear me love.

"She was fifteen years old, so I was convinced that there could be no betrayal in such a youthful soul; since I wouldn't leave her for a mere while, then only, sure of her remarkable steadfastness, I decided to go to the king and ask him to make a try.

"The King, having noticed me, was very happy, for my face was adorned with a victorious smile. He summoned all the ministers and the Grand Vizier and we all walked, rejoicing out loud, to her chambers; but she was nowhere to be found, which filled me with great anxiety, so I asked the old bondwoman where her mistress and my spouse could be. She answered me thus:

'Not even two hours have passed since your spouse escaped with a cameleer, the one that has rheumy eyes and is so strong that he can stop a horse in its gait!'

"Having heard this I swooned, and the king and his ministers started to weep bitterly, for they were very moved at this story and filled with sorrow. King Babu was so sad that having grabbed in desperation, two ministers by their beards, ripped them out completely, then they left to confer and try to reason the cause of this horrible betrayal, but at the end they arrived at nothing, and I, having dropped on my bed, cried for half the year, sometimes ruminating upon the deep matters, exposed to me by my misfortune.

"When I stood before the king again, he shouted of joy, but soon sunk into sorrow, thinking that the second failure is imminent. And so it came, before long, when I married my second wife; she was fat and sedate. I had found such on purpose, thinking that she wouldn't be a frivolous strumpet and prone to betrayal, for I knew that all the greatest calamities are caused by slender women and on thin legs.

"My second wife had no marks on her body, nor warts, which too is a great quality for a woman, who being unable to pride herself with something else, wants to achieve it even with such grace.

"O my friends! Why should I say any more?

"One day we saw, with King Babu, my wife cuddled to her elevated bosom the boy that was very shy, and normally used to shave the king's beard. I had them both killed, and went out to look for a high palm tree, to hang myself on it.

"Nothing else was left for me but death and I had rather chosen death faster than the one awaiting me on order of King Babu. O Akbar Allah! I have seen faithful dogs, I have seen horses, which died of sorrow after their master's death, I have seen a lion that kind as a child, followed its owner, but I have not seen a faithful woman! Tears flew into my eyes, when I recalled my two wives—may the seitan protect them! Would that their souls had no rest after death, and their bodies were eaten by worms! It seemed to me that the entire world was laughing at me, while I walked with silk rope in my hand and my head lifted up, looking for a strong branch to hang myself on. I sat under the palm tree and began to cry, for never before had I been in such dire straits, for at all times before I had hope, but now I had none; I lied on my back, to think—before

I die—about my misfortune and ponder for the last time (even though it would have been of no use at all), what a woman needs to be faithful.

"Night fell, and I mused; night made way for the day, and I mused and examined with thought all that concerned my matter. Finally, my friends, I experienced the miracle: I saw the truth and comprehended that a woman can remain faithful to me. The Prophet has revealed to me what she must be like, to remain so. So I dropped to my face and thanked him, and tears rolled from my eyes, as big as this diamond I had sold to Damascus for thousand ducats, a hundred horses, three hundred camels and a hundred bondmaids. I presented the silk rope that was about to cause my death, to a passer-by, who walking slowly, stared at the palm trees, just like I had, the day before. Then, having stood before King Babu, I spoke boldly:

'My worthy Lord, I shall tie the knot for the third time today.'

"Wondered king Babu, for he had nothing else to do at the moment, and answered me favourably:

'After your death I shall have only one of your eyes taken out, for you are a miserable man. God is one!'

"And I set out inland and after many weeks, I brought in a sedan chair, the third wife, since she was tired, I laid her down on the sofa and prostrated before her; I clad her in grandest silks, I had various incenses burnt in her chamber and was asking her fondly, how much she loved me, she would not answer, but stare at me, very emphatically.

"I was very happy when I stood before King Babu that was just pouring his tears into the malachite vase, which he was doing daily, for two hours before the sunset, for at other times he used to be very busy with state affairs. I waited very patiently for King Babu to stop crying, then having dropped to my knees I called out:

'May Allah give you as many lands as the sun beholds and as numerous people as the stars you see. May he give you eternal felicity and joy of soul, strength of a lion and wits of a fox, O Babu! O Immortal King!'

"This said, I started to prostrate and as the custom was, I hit the ground with my forehead seventy-seven times, and King Babu looked at me favourably and wondered exceedingly, thinking that I was coming to ask him for the sparing of my life. Therefore he asked:

'Have you, miserable Sindbad, been betrayed by your third wife yet?'

"I answered him:

'Rejoice your heart, Sultan, for I have found in your land a woman that shall be famous throughout the world, for she is a faithful wife that no other can be found under the sun.'

'How will you convince me of this, Sindbad, so that I cheer up and stop crying and mourning eternally?'

'Order, my lord!' I said.

"King Babu ordered that we hide behind a curtain, and instructed all the mighty of his land and all the most handsome youths to appear before her in turns and try to seduce her. I showed anxiety, but willingly agreed and having approached my wife, quietly resting on a silk sofa, I spoke out, so that everyone could hear me:

'I bid you goodbye, my beloved wife, rose from Allah's gardens, star leading the sailors, for I am leaving with King Babu for a hunt and for three days you will be left alone.'

"Then having stooped, I kissed her lovingly, took my quiver and left, my step steady. I hid with the king behind a curtain and looked what was about to happen. And then, for three days and three nights, proceeded and stood before her, all whom the king ordered to do so.

"The brother of the king arrived first; a mighty lord, although he had a squint, and tempted her saying:

'I have brought you strands of pearls and handfuls of rubies. Come with me!'

"But she, not even uttering a word, was lying silent and serene.

"Then came the ministers, their words sleek and crafty, each of them promising her things so marvellous that uneasiness grabbed at my heart, but she remained so cold that King Babu marvelled.

"Then the strongest man in the kingdom arrived and having delivered to her short and crude speech, he tightened his muscles, thus exposing to her eyes thighs resembling oaks, and arms like knotty clubs, able to kill many. Oh my friends! I was afraid of this man most of all, but still he withdrew with shame and disgrace, for she, my most faithful spouse, did not even deign to glimpse at his magnificent body.

'I think, I am going to smile!' whispered King Babu to me and stared in great admiration, for just then a man with a scroll of sheepskin in his hand sneaked into her fragrant chamber, lit with a lamp, and having kneeled on his right knee, started to read long poems, of such miraculous beauty that they brought tears to my eyes, but she not even sighed, filling everyone with wonder.

"Two hundred knights and hundred poets had already shamefully withdrawn, departed in disgrace princes and ministers, dervishes and other rabble, for the king ordered that everyone tried to seduce her. When finally spake king Babu:

'It is strange and yet unseen in this world, but I shall admit your victory, Sindbad, only if she resists me!'

"This heard, I dropped to his feet and begged him not to do it, for there is no woman in this world that would resist him, ruler of half of the world and three-fifths of the moon, for all the rest belongs to the Caliph of Baghdad. He answered though that it could not be another way, and having entered her chamber, he stood in a bright circle of the lamp and spake mightily:

'I am the fearful and wise King Babu, before whom lightning trembles and storm crawls like a dog. Listen to me, Sindbad's wife: if you let me into your bed, I shall make you my wife, I shall give you as many riches as you might fancy, and have Sindbad hanged, to please you. Answer me, and I shall make you happy!'

"King Babu waited for her answer, and for a moment it seemed to me that she moved; it was only a phantasm though, for after a little while, King Babu returned. He hugged and kissed me, weeping with joy; his heart filled with pride and delight, for the sun shone again in his eyes on account of me.

"He asked me, what was it that I desired, and I answered that I wanted to come back to my homeland with my faithful wife.

"Then he summoned all his ministers and said: 'Here is my friend!'

"And he had me honoured, like no one had been honoured before in this country; gave me ship and slaves, many golden chains and silver pitchers, elegant garments, spangled with diamonds, grandest weapons, and let me set sail for my homeland. Ashore stood all his people and cheered, and when this grandest treasure—my faithful wife—was carried in a sedan chair, the crowd whipped itself into a frenzy, and King Babu rejoiced like never before.

"I returned to Baghdad, for once again the Prophet saved me and let me acquire immense riches, worth a thousandfold the wood and saffron, devoured by the sea!"

He took a breath and beheld his friends, who all wondered greatly and it seemed that none of them wanted to believe the tale, so odd and unheard-of since the beginning of the world, but seaman Sindbad, seeing that they were finding it hard to believe, said:

"To bear witness to the truth, I am going to show you my spouse, most faithful that ever was, and faithful to me until this day."

He clapped his hands, and four slaves brought in woman on a chair padded with purple.

"Here she is, my friends!" said Sindbad.

They bowed down their heads low, greeting her, and started to stare at her from the corner of their eyes, with interest, seeing with difficulty, for the chamber was dark and filled with olive lamp smoke.

All of a sudden unease reflected on one of the faces.

"Allah Rossoulah!" they began repeating in amazement.

Then they shouted:

"Sindbad! This woman is dead!"

And wise seaman Sindbad smiled craftily, quietly stroking his beard, and said:

"You fools! How on earth could she otherwise remain faithful for so long!"

They pondered hard, and eventually everyone admitted, in their hearts that his words are swollen with great wisdom like dumpy sacks, swollen with grain.

Finally one of them said:

"You embalmed her, Sindbad, and you know that she won't betray you. Why have you veiled her face then?"

"For one cannot be certain of a woman, even after her death!" he answered and was saddened, for experienced a lot, and suffered a lot had the wise seaman Sindbad.

Gentle Virgin and a Horse

It is a thing worth wondering about, even for the greatest sage, sitting on a divan and scratching scabies from a lofty chest, ruminating a lot; or a crafty barber who had heard many stories from people that had arrived from far and wide: how much the moon is similar to a jackal, stars to lizards twinkling with gold, clouds to dromedaries, and sun to a man. This can even be understood by a man, who by nature, is as stupid as an ostrich and in his childhood had been heavily beaten on the head with a bamboo stick, and even a man of contemptible trade—a cobbler or even one that writes poems; it also happened that a woman, having contemplated it deeply and for some time, her thoughts not flying off sideways (like a crossbreed of donkey and a mule that without good cause, hee-hawing loudly, its tail upturned, dashes away from the herd) will understand that many things in the sky are similar to things in the world—mangy and trivial.

That is how Ibrahim deeply pondered, son of Yusuf and one baker, both loved by his noble mother, who was right in thinking that two men would manage to get the job done faster and more sensibly than just one. Maybe that was the reason that Ibrahim was so skilled in thinking, deep and exceptional, and people's respect followed him like jackal follows the camel. Not many people knew him though—three at the most, Kadi from Damascus included that tried him once for theft of a turnip and cutting a purebred mare's tail. It's better for a man though, if his name is respected by a handful of people, rather than being disdained by a thousand—like this Baghdad sage, who, being able to taste great respect, due to his excessive intellect earned people's contempt, because he got married for the twenty-seventh time, when, by a lucky accident, he was abandoned by his twenty-sixth wife, the daughter of a cobbler and a saitan at the same time, termagant and a fury. So it happens at times that by inconceivable decrees of a Prophet, sometimes a sage is more similar to a lame donkey, than a donkey is to a sage.

And so it happened that greatly people-respected Ibrahim was alone in El Haazar oasis, for the tribe inhabiting it had just set out for horse stealing, which they used to do with great fantasy and adequate skill, for there's nothing worse than doing one's thing carelessly and indolently; therefore rightly wise man turns his back on a thief that got himself caught, although it can also be that a thief dislikes to look another thief in the eyes. Based on this notion, one could also tell why half of the people on this earth look down at the ground.

Ibrahim, son of Yusuf (and one baker), was just looking in the sky, resting, for he was very tired. He held an important and urgent office, for his thing was to raise water out of the earth's stomach, which he did all day long, sustained by turning the waterwheel that pulled up buckets of water from the well's abyss. Although one doesn't need much learning or cunning for this trade, it can only be done by a man who's sedate, whose thoughts aren't dispersed, and who manages to go round from sunrise to sunset. Sometimes it seemed to him, when his mind turned so much that it became hot pilau; that he himself is the well and out of himself draws tasty water. Despite that though, the man respected his work, rightly thinking that even a greatest sage does nothing more than going in circles, raising water later drunk by people and mangy, squealing mules. For his work he wasn't rewarded much, because, apart from receiving two handfuls of dates, he could drink as much water as he liked, for it's just and fair thing that one can fully consume the fruits of his labour.

His greatest remuneration though, was his buoyancy—a great and priceless treasure, for Ibrahim had sky in his chest and in his head constantly, and because of thinking of it all day long, he had water. His thoughts were therefore pure and elevated; he was also aware of many things, inconceivable to others, as the one that he was contemplating at the moment, lying on his dignified, only scarcely ulcerated back. Looking at the sun, he saw that it was a warrior mounting a fiery horse of great price and great blood that dashes across the sky's desert. Sometimes he stops, his horse drinking water out of the black cloud, full like a goatskin sack, then having cried out loudly, the warrior dashes again to Medina of the West, where he's awaited by a Prophet sitting on a purple divan made of soft clouds, and smoking hookah as big as a palm tree; its smoke descending on the earth like a silvery mist. There the sunny warrior drops to the ground before the Prophet, who, very content, let's him kiss his foot and says: "Rest overnight at the harem, for tomorrow you shall hasten to the East, to carry my blessing."

That is what Ibrahim thought, lying in people's respect on a dignified back, when suddenly he started to listen carefully, for with his trained, albeit dirty ear, he caught the sound of the tramp of a horse. At this moment, being of very sharp mind, he nimbly realized that, if horse's hooves can be heard, then someone's coming up. Having jumped to his feet, he started to turn the waterwheel that creaked in a strange voice that could be understood, like that of a jackal barking hoarsely or quarrelsome woman starting to speak.

Right in front of him someone halted the horse so abruptly that the hooves threw up clods of earth. The steed was beautiful like a houri, as black as night, his eyes like two twinkling stars. Having smelled a man, he widened his nostrils and sat back on his haunches, just as a princess would who, wanting to appear more beauteous, leans back sweetly, thus showing the exuberance of her breasts, as abundant and fertile as a sultan's gardens, full like leather sacks of wine; still aflame with gait, the gorgeous steed trembled like an odalisque, led into Caliph's bed, anxiously hoping her body is fragrant enough. Then the horse, having smelt the water, started to flick his ears like a dervish—heaven suddenly opened before him, for he had smelt cooked hen through the wall.

Ibrahim gazed in awe at the noble animal and wisely thought from the depth of his soul that many things in this world are more beautiful than a man; a notion he found even easier to believe in, when he looked on the rider that harmed the noble steed, riding on it with such a face. It was similar to a rotten melon, out of which looked the eyes, rancid like fusty pilau, phoney and sly. The rider's loathsome gob was scarcely adorned by a beard, similar to an old jackal's mangy tail with its coat fallen out, and not enough of it left to accommodate the many fleas in its thicket.

The rider, having watched Ibrahim, waved at him to come closer, then having at close quarters smeared him with his slimy sight, asked:

"Is your water good for drinking?"

"Is your horse wise?" Ibrahim answered sensibly.

"My horse is wise like grand vizier, and cunning like a dervish."

"Why do you ask then, if the water is good, seeing how your horse flicks his ears out of joy at the sight of it?"

"Allah!" said the rider, "You speak reason. Do you scoop your wisdom from the well? Give me a drink." Ibrahim thought for a while; then, having looked at him oddly, he spake:

"Has your horse carried you, or have you carried the horse? Therefore I will water your horse first."

"The horse will neither smash your head, nor call you son of swain. I can easily do the former and the latter, though."

"You rightly say," answered Ibrahim sweetly, "Therefore I will water your horse first."

This said, he took a goatskin, scooped the water, and smiling invitingly, like a bridegroom on the day of his wedding, he watered the steed, which drank greedily and with pleasure, squinting his eyes and flicking his ears. Then he snorted and shuddered, like a man that just came out of a bath and greatly refreshed, looks at the world more cheerfully.

Ibrahim gazed at all that, clucking his mouth joyfully, like an old ulcerated pasha, promenading slowly down the line of virgins (more or less defiled) offered for sale; who sometimes, for greater contentment, pretends that he wants to buy a gorgeous Greek girl just grown from puberty, being unable to arouse his heart dried and barren, similar to an empty bag that used to contain a lot, with something more lively, and claps her lightly on the shoulder blade or holding her by the chin, strokes her face with his second hand. That is how Ibrahim, with great contentment, touched the black, shiny, and soft coat of the horse and was carefully repelling flies off his neck, similar to the neck of the Sultan's daughter, whose father had his eunuchs strangle her, for she had an offspring with a whirling dervish. No harm happened to her though, for as one famous poet said (that later lost his mind out of excessive admiration)—her neck was so beautiful that whichever eunuch touched it, he would feel suddenly, by inconceivable thing of a Prophet, such passions and might, such affection and love that he would rather hang himself, than harm her. This is how three-hundred ninety and nine of them died; the last one saved by the desperate Sultan, so that this useful male species didn't extinct completely.

"What is your horse's name?" Ibrahim finally asked.

"He goes by the name of Ostrich Son, meaning he can surpass the wind in the desert. This horse runs faster than death that was chasing me recently mounting a samum, and having failed to catch me, is now biting sand in the desert out of despair and jerking his beard in anger. You tell me though, what I owe you for the water, for I am not a dignitary of a kind that doesn't pay and kicks out teeth!" Ibrahim weighed the thing long and hard in his thoughts. Then he spake:

"If your favour is small like a date's stone, give me a copper coin, and be sure that I won't curse you, wish you broken legs, or getting choked on a sheep's bone. If your favour is big as a mosque, then let me, for my water, ride on your horse from this palm to the other one nearby that shrivelled, for one sage hanged himself on it recently. Why are you laughing?"

"It seemed to me that you are sensible, but you are stupid just like an ostrich egg. You want me to let you ride my horse? Ohe, ohe! Don't you know that a horse of great blood is seven times more honest than a woman that having no great heart and not considering her master, will perpetrate every possible betrayal? Even if I let you on the horse's back, it would be better for you to sit on an iron pot filled with burning coals, for you would manage to sit on it longer. I won't let you though, for you might escape. Having stolen the horse myself, I know how easily it's done. At that time one could mount it though, but today the horse, having understood who his rightful owner is, would break all your ribs, if kawas wouldn't do it in jail."

This said, he jumped off the saddle and having led the horse to the palm tree, he tied him to it, then having sat comfortably, watched Ibrahim with malice. The latter lowered his head on his chest, which not having to carry very heavy burden, breathed fast. He too sat on the hard base of his legs and remained silent, thinking that there's nothing more to be said. The former having eaten several dates, which he chewed long, then spat them in his hand, then dried them in sun's swelter and started to chew again, was musing upon something, waggling sensibly, like the great sage-elephant does; he squinted his musty eyes, then opened them again, like a camel dying of age, then, having evenly fed his stomach and heart, commenced a somewhat strange conversation with Ibrahim.

"What is your name? he asked him first.

"Ibrahim, Yusuf's son," he answered.

"Your name is splendid. Greetings to you, Ibrahim." The latter wondered.

"Why are you greeting me only now?"

"Because I can see that you aren't money-greedy and you didn't want it for the water. You are prudent too, Ibrahim, Yusuf's son, would that he lived hundred years."

"He is dead already; why don't you leave him alone?"

"Then, if he lived, would that he lived three times one hundred years. You can see for yourself, how much you fit my heart; if I had a son, I would like him to be like you."

"Do not say it, for I would have to wish you to be like my father that lies in his grave."

"Bismillah! Your father is in heaven."

"You said! My father has never stolen a horse."

That is how they conversed with one another, for it was clear that the rider was awaiting something and in the meantime exercised his mind in great thinking and trained his tongue like a warrior that before going to battle, swings long his curved sabre, crying loudly to encourage his heart that knows no fear; being sensible though, it knows that all the clamour will help it a lot. A long moment passed, before he said:

"Ibrahim, Yusuf's son, wasn't Abdul Azeez riding here on a camel—a friend of mine and a relative—but at the same time a great thief and uncle of a jackal?"

"No such person was here. Why?"

"For if he wasn't, it means he will be, and having business with this man I am afraid that he might attack and rob me, for the man dares everything. I therefore ask you Ibrahim, to pay attention and defend me should the necessity arise."

"What is your business with him?"

"This man wants to buy this horse off me."

"What did you say?"

"He wants to buy this horse off me."

"The Caliph will buy this horse, when he finds out about it."

"The Caliph won't pay me what Abdul Azeez will pay."

"Allah! Your mind is disturbed."

"Why are you hurting me? Look at me and realize that I could, with one hit of my fist, beat out your eye and knock out three-times-ten teeth, but I am gracious, seeing that you love my horse."

"More than you."

"The Prophet will pay you for this with hard and deadly disease, or leprosy, or decaying liver. Now listen, for it seems to me that two camels can be seen on the horizon. There he comes up, would that he never came. Do you know what he wants to give me for my horse?"

"My ears are wide like gates of Baghdad."

"He wants to give me his daughter. Oh!" Having said that, he squinted his eyes mustily, with an oily smile, widely opening a slimy snout, out of which lots of saliva trickled down his scarce beard, sure sign that his soul is in bliss and beholds heavens.

Ibrahim mused sadly, seeming to weigh some deep thoughts, for in his eyes he had great concern that sat on his face, between the eyes like an evil, wild bird that sat on a tree and tears the bark with his claw. One could clearly see though that he feels great contempt for his comrade, and in his good soul compares him to horse's manure.

The latter woke from his delight and noticing the comers are close, silently called the horse by its name, then stood up, walked a couple of steps and waited, till he felt near him the fast and wheezing breathing of winded camels, similar to the sighs, heaved out of the breast of an old and fat woman, suddenly embraced with the flame of desire. Then he grabbed both camels by their harnesses—very stinky, for they were soaked with old, fusty oil for better flexibility; and with strong hand forced the camels to kneel, which they did, gazing sensibly and sadly, for there are two sad things in this world: the two eyes of a camel.

Abdul Azeez jumped on the ground; a scoundrel tall like a palm tree, his snout cheeky, black as a seitan's; his eyes squinting and very unquiet, so it seemed he sees everything at once and would like to steal all he sees. Following him, reeling after the fast camel's gait, was a woman, her face covered with charshaf; of shapely figure and supple, which you can easily recognize, if with wise eye you manage to see through thick broadcloth clothes, although another sage claims that it's easier to discover what's inside the earth than uncover the defects of a horse or a woman. Even the Prophet doesn't know it.

The woman stood silent, and they were greeting each other beautifully, using words tasty and comely, as becomes of men of whom Allah only knows that both of them are pretty considerable thieves. Thus spake Abdul Azeez:

"For thirty days now, I've been wishing you luck and that your stomach be never ailed, Mohammed, my brother, brilliance of my days. Would that you never see the jackal of sadness and the snake of worry, and let your sabre fulfil great deeds. Only one thing surprises me, is that you aren't a Caliph, for you should be it!

This said he looked at his friend as one looks at a rotten egg or an eelworm or carrion. The latter, named Mohammed, spat on him in the depth of his abysmal thought, kicked him secretly in his stomach and having thought that even a jackal wouldn't touch this bandit, for so horribly he smells of thief, he walked slowly and with dignity on paradisiacal meadow of his soul and picked flowers of his words, smelling of incense. This is what he said:

"If Aladdin entered your heart, he would have been surprised seeing the treasures, which even a hundred earthly Sultans don't have. I know that Allah loves you for it, for tonight he said to the Prophet: 'Tell me, has the sun fallen down on the ground, or is this Abdul Azeez walking the earth?' For that, would that he gave you life twice as long as I wish you, friend of mine, whom I love. I said." Then, having sat before each other, they looked each other long in the eyes, and they knew what they knew. And when a long moment passed, walking on crutches spoke Mohammed, as if not knowing how things are:

"Has the angel Gabriel arrived with you on the second camel?"

"This is my daughter," answered Abdul Azeez modestly, "Who loves you, of which I know for sure. Now, tell me, who is this man that's not looking at us but at your horse. Don't you reckon that he will enchant your horse, and even without this your horse is not as sound, as you might think." Mohammed answered slowly, his face reddened:

"It's a man that raises buckets of water, and so sensible is the man that he'd rather look at my horse than at your daughter."

"If he is so sensible, his eye might easily flow out, if I approach him."

"Abdul Azeez, the man is so wise that he prefers to have just one eye, in order not to see with his two eyes that your daughter lacks seven teeth from the very front."

The former's liver stung and spilled some bile, but he played it cool, he even smiled the smile of a half-mad man, and said:

"I know that you like joking, my brother. Oh, I am having such a grand laugh! For the laugh I would forget to tell you that Al Mahar's minister gives me thirty camels and six-times-one hundred rams for her."

"And you didn't go to see the Caliph?"

"What for?"

"To tell him that his minister went mad. And if not, why didn't you take what was offered to you?"

"Because I want to have your horse whose tail is very beautiful. Everything else about the horse is ordinary and cheap; I want to treat you like a brother though and therefore ask you fair and square, will you give me the horse in exchange for my daughter, would that she served you for thousand years?"

Mohammed didn't say a word, but having risen with dignity, approached the woman, and having opened her mouth, started to count her teeth diligently, then having fingered a wisp of her hair, he tried its softness, as one tries silks at Baghdad bazaar. His musty face got longer and longer, then he touched her breasts, checked her hands, then having stood behind her, carefully measured the position of her shoulder blades, and finally, acting somewhat immodestly, he examined all her body curves. This done, he sat back again quietly and said:

"No I won't!"

Abdul Azeez stabbed him with his eyes, like with a dagger and smiled.

"What do you want for your horse then?"

"Firstly, your daughter."

"I have given her to you already."

"Both camels will be mine."

"Eh?"

"You shall also give me this sabre and two daggers of damascene steel."

"What did you say?"

"You shall give me two saddles, and each year, until ten years have passed, ten rams to feed her, for she is thin."

Abdul Azeez goggled his eyes and it seemed he went mad; he panted so heavily, as if a sandstorm was coming from the desert, then, having caught his breath, he reddened and said as if through tears:

"My daughter has face of the sun."

"My horse," answered Mohammed, "doesn't cover his face."

"She loves you like a pupil of an eye."

"Ask my horse, if he is not capable of doing the same?"

"Mohammed! Have you ever seen a woman with legs so shapely and beautiful?"

"She has only two legs, while my horse has four."

"Bismillah!" groaned Abdul Azeez. "Her voice is like that of a nightingale."

"You want to deceive me then; my horse doesn't speak at all. Now, let me tell you this: he won't wish me death; he won't betray me and won't curse me. My horse is sensible and neither needs damask for clothing, nor sandals, nor delicacies. Neither he cries nor laughs. Do you see now how much you wanted to trick me, you great thief, you son of Ali Baba? Will you give camels, sabre, saddles, and rams?"

"I won't!" roared Abdul Azeez. He jumped up and grabbed his friend by his scarce beard; the latter did the same, but more greedily, and they started to wallow on the ground, tearing out each other's hair, quite fairly and evenly. The woman shouted and jumped to the camels, but the men, oblivious to everything around them, banged their pates against bellies, twisted their arms and bit each other with decayed teeth. When their powers finally left them, they retreated from each other, panting heavily and belching out words, stinky and decayed. But suddenly their swarthy faces paled and pupils widened.

"What is this?" groaned Mohammed. Abdul Azeez looked long, and finally having comprehended, shouted scarily:

"The man raising buckets has snatched the horse, camels, and my daughter and is running away!"

"Allah Rossoulah!"

Mohammed jumped to his feet and having clutched at his head, he shook it like a stone. His friend stared long at the runaway, and finally sweetly spake:

"You said Mohammed that he's a sensible man... But what is this?"

Mohammed gazed too. The man stopped afar off, not being afraid of a chase, and then slowly raised the veil from the face of Abdul Azeez's daughter; and one could see from the distance that suddenly, as if hit by a lightning, he grabbed her by the arms, took her off the camel and sped away like a wind—while she, with great cry, was coming back to her father's bosom, his eyes popped wide out of desperation. Mohammed beheld him and spake:

"You said he's a sensible man?"

"I'm telling you, he's a *sage*, you thief, you son and grandson of a thief."

Murder of Harun ar Rashid

The son of Mahdi grew very weary, a just Caliph, Harun ar Rashid, for all day long he was receiving a deputation of Christian Sultan, an immensely famous man, despite him being an infidel and drinking wine; he heard envoys standing in grand retinue leaning against their heavy swords, many times repeat the name "ar Rashid" and each time bowing down their heads with respect. Those were the knights so magnificent, so that it wasn't a retinue that was stood in ar Rashid's throne hall, but an oakwood that with Merlin's spell sprouted from great marble flagstones. They had buff hair and huge moustaches resembling rather horse tails than facial adornment, their chests broad like mosques, clad in excellent armour or leather, so shiny that watching from afar, one could think they are lions that having shaken their mane, rose to hind legs, ready to maul everything that stands before them. Their eyes were glaring and ruffianly, as if soaked with blood, but Harun ar Rashid quickly realized that having noticed his immense riches, they grew bigger and bigger and more amazed, so he decided to dim them even more and ordered to exhibit even more riches, so that their knightly minds almost boiled at the sight of carpets as patterned as a meadow on the Normandy coast; armours so grand that not even an archangel endues for a battle with saitan; immeasurable quantities of diamonds and pearls, and many, many other miracles that one cannot find even in a spell-bound cave.

So they wondered mightily and dented the marble floor with their swords, and their souls came out of their chests, where their hard and dark abode was, and hung on the lashes of stunned eyes.

But even though Harun had golden vats and golden plates, fancifully shaped goblets and even more immeasurable wealth brought out, he didn't manage to show them everything, for the sun transformed from the diamond into a yellow topaz, and after a while it dripped with blood like from a ruby, before the black agate of the night twinkled with eerie glow. It would take many days that the slaves, wiping sweat from their foreheads after hard work, managed to take out of the treasuries all that slept a golden dream there, under the guard of hundred locks and tens of lions that were chained to the wall and starved, walked to and fro before the treasury doors. So motioned the just Caliph, to give rest to the tired eyes, and having dipped his hands into a big leather pail, in which pearls fantasized a rainbow reverie about a seabed, he brought them out by the handfuls and poured into the helmets of the knightly bevy of king Charlemagne, as if he poured peas. Then, very content, he motioned one of the courtiers and said graciously:

"Order that each of these noble knights is given a woman for tonight. Let them tell, in their country later that in Baghdad there are magnificent men, and women resembling flowers."

"Your Highness!" flabbergasted the dignitary.

"Why do you blench?"

"My Lord!" says he, "It shall happen as you wish; but before you order again, turn your noble eyes on them. Even an anatolian mare would not suffice for each of these terrifying giaurs[*], bigger than the mountain. Is it your desire then that they reduced these slender

---

[*] infidel – non Muslim.

virgins of princely families, to shreds, for each of them shall die tomorrow after this ordeal?"

And Harun, being immensely favourable, ordered:

"You shall give each of them two then."

"Too few!" whispered back the dignitary, measuring them once again with his inquisitive eye.

"Give each of them four then!" said the Caliph, whom they honoured, shouting in such voice that a crash produced by mountain top collapsing and falling into the chasm is a mere whisper compared to it, when the learned interpreter explained them, how great the Caliph's favour was. Then their moustaches ruffled, and legs started to quiver, one could also hear, as their hearts started to pound against the armour plates, as if they were eagles closed in iron cages. Then they fast withdrew, to anoint their hair with oil, to appear worthily before Sultan's princesses, and Harun ar Rashid breathed with relief and with nod of his head bade his cortege goodbye. Then, having turned his eyes to his spouse, noticed that her eyes are half-angry and half-sad. He said then:

"Why are you sad, noble Zobeida?"

She did not say a word though, but having bowed down, left; and retreating slowly to her chambers, she thought that big and strong must be love of a giaur, whose arms resemble the knotty clubs, and thighs the boughs of an oak. She was very sad and cried all night, ruminating upon various matters, and sometimes she would sigh heavily, strangely imagining something.

43

The Caliph had his excellent garments taken off, one similar to sunrise and the other to sunset, he unbelted a dagger, resembling a serpent glittering with rainbow, and unbelted the sword, resembling the lightning; he felt great relief when the dexterous servant took off his head a turban, playing with colours grander than paradisiacal bird or bouquet of flowers from sultan's gardens, and sighed relief once again, like a man that finished hard work. One could already feel a fresh breeze of the night, of which the Caliph used to say that she is his most favourite of the virgins, for he was able to learn a lot in its silence and spot in its darkness, what was invisible for the others. Today too, he thought that most enjoyable rest would be leaving the palace secretly (as he did many times before) and going to the streets of Baghdad, where strange things took place, of which had known neither Mahdi, his noble father, nor Al Jafar, going by the name of Al Mansur, the even nobler father of his noble father. Many a time, having come out incognito to the streets of his city, he listened what its great mouth, consisting of many thousands of lips had to say, and would always hear such word that was more similar to truth than a diamond to a teardrop. Ar Rashid trembled at its sight, although only half of his soul was just; the other though, had evil eyes and hollow thoughts, as it often happens with souls of those, whom Allah gave royalty and sceptre; he would rather watch the blood than tears trickling down a human's face and carving furrows, as eternal water drops carving the white marble; then he would squint his eyes, and gloom would fall upon just half of his soul and he got very sad, as if tears were burning him.

On his finger he had a ring that sometimes would shine like a sunray, when suddenly, like a lightning, it hits a diamond and failing to scratch, it only sparks grand fire out of its hardness, and thousand glitters. In the gemstone of the ring a teardrop was closed, and when he was asked:

"Grand Caliph, what shines in your ring?"

"Poison!" would answer Harun ar Rashid. Then everyone would think in depth of their souls: Wary is the Caliph and carries poison on him, just in case. What is he afraid of, he who is just?"

And he mused, when he managed to hide his face from people's eyes, how to make, in his city and his land alike, all the tears dry up, only one left, closed forever in shiny gemstone, contained therein and unable to spread like a locust, for nothing spreads as easily as tears. His worry therefore grew stronger and stronger, although he knew that Allah manages to dry up a sea, but even he is not capable of drying up people's tears. The curse is even greater than the might of Allah; for whenever Allah reaps tears from the great field, having dispatched the sun to do this job, as many new seitan shall sow at night, and in the morning, the mouldy ear of sorrow and suffering has already grown; and so the struggle continues from the beginning of the world and it shall never stop, for one dreadful day even Allah will doubt, and start crying out of great sorrow himself. Then, end of the world shall come, for had the moon, breaking off the celestial dome, crashed onto earth's surface, the world would not collapse into the great sea of darkness, in which it floats on back of a fish, but should even one tear of God drop upon it, the world would fall, like a stone falling into the abyss.

Many times had Harun mused upon it before, especially, when the night, wearing a starry turban, descended on earth like a musing pilgrim that vowed silence and had his tongue cut out, to fulfil his vows. Even now he was thinking of things, on which ordinary man would not ponder and rather escape from, like from death or bubonic plague. He reckoned that he should be firm for these who are weak, and should care for those that shiver, thinking of death or a great suffering. He used to, having recognized it by pale and miserable face, never turn back on it, stop kindly, wanting to comfort it, but as the two slaves, standing at the palace's gates with spears in their hands, would chase all the misery away, therefore the Caliph would go out into the streets of his capital and searched for suffering, in the curing of which he would find strange relief and joy to his heart.

When he thought what immense riches, the foreign envoys saw this day in his palace, he trembled, thinking to himself, what great poverty they could see outside the palace gates, having descended to the river that had a morbid breath. He squinted his eyes for a moment and having sighed, said to himself: "I shall go and see, if the river is not swollen with tears" Then he clapped his hands and ordered the servant that appeared:

"Make me a noble Persian, who arrived to Baghdad to catch a glimpse of Rashid and cheat on weight of wool."

The crafty servant understood the Caliph's wish like a shot, and started to clothe him ably, being accustomed to his master's whims; he clad him in yellow robes, girded with broche belt, and having put on his head a turban made of the same fabric, sprinkled his beard with the scarlet dust, so that he, smelling beautifully, looked excessively noble. When he had finished, ar Rashid girded himself with a curved sabre hanging on silk tapes, then having grabbed in his right hand a long staff with an ivory knob, he put behind his belt a pouch, full of golden coins, and left through the secret door, through which, sometimes at night, corpses were brought out, if a woman died in the palace, for the men would die either in fierce combat or at the baths, hit with a sudden death of excessive heat.

He was swept by the chill that hatched by the river, and the light breeze shook down some of the scarlet dust of the Caliph's beard; Harun thought for a while, which way to go, then nobly and without a hurry, as becomes a rich wool merchant, he entered—having passed few empty squares—the narrow streets, from whence, at this very moment, a stinky odour crawled out, and failing to spare his noble nostrils, started to tickle them. Ar Rashid stepped out and after a while he mixed with people that after a sweltering day crowded out onto the streets to catch some fresh air that was thick and muggy, but still nicer than in stone houses.

He was stopping here and there, looking with interest at whatever happened, drawing from it many conclusions, for a sensible man shall not go past even a stone without noticing something of value in it, what someone else cannot see, despite passing it, day in day out for a hundred years. For ar Rashid reckoned that there is no such thing on earth on which one could not see a touch of Allah's finger and one tiny moment of his meditation, therefore everything should be respected, save for a woman, for it is true that Allah did not set his hand to this doing of an evil spirit, therefore she bears no trace of divine touch. The Caliph stopped, looking, as six men held a ram by its legs and horns, one of them trying to cut its throat, but either the knife was blunt or he acted lumpishly, so he rested once in a while, addressing the others:

"The meat is going to be bad, for this ram is tough!"

Then he would butcher it with great strength and concentration, the others beheld his labour and were eating the ram with their eyes, very greedily, lovingly listening to its painful baaing; and in a little while they would chase it with a great cry, for breaking loose, it was running away, until it banged its head against the wall and became dazed.

47

Elsewhere, Harun ar Rashid could see a woman milking the goat that, believing in kismet, stood motionless, cunningly spacing her hind legs, eleven kids waiting for its milk, frozen in expectation. Then he would stare with great curiosity, how a woman, sitting on a doorstep was searching for vermin on her husband's head, and a little boy, putting them on a stone, was labouriously killing them with a hit of another stone.

"My people are sloppy," thought Caliph, but he didn't become angry, but very worried and walked on, avoiding the puddles and big dogs sleeping in the middle of the road.

When he started his descent towards the river, he heard great clamour in front of a shabby stone house, and many people bent to the ground, were groaning very severely; so he came closer and asked what the reason of the tumult was.

"One man is dying here in great pain."

"Has the death counted up his years and told him that he lived too long?"

"You are foreign here, apparently Persian, so you do not know that no one in Baghdad dies hoary"

"How did you say?"

"I said that no one here, starving, can reach hoary age."

"Is this man dying of starvation?"

"You missed—this man is dying of surfeit."

"Eh?" wondered the Caliph.

"Having no flour, and out of desperation, he ate soil today, to cheat his stomach, and apparently he has eaten too much of it, for he is dying now; thus, about to eat soil again."

"Kismet!"

Harun ar Rashid stood motionless, for he froze in pain; he had to lean on his ebony staff not to reel back, and stared, terrified at the thin, livid man, whose hands chained with cramp were scratching the paving stones.

"Why are you so surprised?" asked his interlocutor, "Doesn't anyone die in your country?"

"But not of starvation," answered the Caliph. "Why did not this man go to see the Caliph, who would feed him?"

"Do you know why the Caliph didn't come to see him?"

"I do not know, forsooth."

And with his hands trembling, he started to produce a pouch from behind his belt and having taken out several pieces of gold, he said quietly:

"Give it to him from me."

"Give it to him yourself, if you reckon that death can be bribed with a coin. Why didn't you come earlier?"

Harun ar Rashid stood for a while, not considering that the gold slipped out of his hand, then with great effort, he turned back and left this place slowly, stooped, as if he carried the man that has just died, on his own shoulders. Everyone was stepping aside with respect, considering his dignified posture and rich attire, but he, noticing no one, walked on and on. Sometimes hearing the acute cry of a baby, he would step out, stopping his ears with his hands. Suddenly he had to stop, for in the middle of the street stood a donkey, spacing its legs, and under it, like under a movable roof, a man was lying, a stone under his head.

"Why don't you let me go?" he addressed the man kindly.

"Why don't you let me sleep?" answered the other.

Harun ar Rashid stared at him attentively.

"Don't you have home, to sleep in?"

"Am I a Caliph, to have a home? Forgive me, my lord that I have not raised, to bow down before you, for I can see, you are gracious, but my legs are swollen, I have been standing in water all day."

"What do you do?"

"I bring out the mud, where the dam is about to be built, then I put two baskets on my donkey and heave one on my back."

"Do you always sleep under your donkey?"

"Not always, for sometimes it lies down as well." Rashid asked no more, but drew out a piece of gold again, and said, stooping over the lying man:

"Take this from me."

"What are you giving me, gold? Had you several dates, I would take them willingly, but gold is of no use for me. Had I shown it to anyone, I would receive lashes, for I would be accused of stealing them, and my donkey is not of a kind that lays gold. Happy journey, foreigner."

"May Allah protect you!"

"Do not remind Allah of me," answered the other, "for if he spots me, he will send rain for me not to sleep in the street."

Harun gazed at this strange man for another, long while, and even more thoughtful than before, he approached the great bridge that he commissioned not so long ago. Great hustle and bustle could be heard from there, for always on the river, people gathered in greater numbers, as if thinking that the waters shall bring them something good from afar. Many bazaars were located here, already closed at this time of the day, and many tents of travelling merchants, causing great hubbub at daytime, and even greater at night, for being in a foreign city, everyone got very frightened, and therefore shouted as loud as possible, so that everybody knew that he is brave and scared of no one. Here too, by the bridge's entrance odalisques were sold, so the crowd was massive, maybe even bigger than at the horse market in the eastern part of a city, especially with night approaching, for the women, expensive in daytime, could be bought cheaper toward the evening, for everybody knows that every commodity is cheaper before shop closing, and the merchants praised and shouted most loudly at dusk, thinking cunningly that in the dark it is easier to sell a woman defiled multiple times or having many defects in her posture. Just by the bridge, on the protruding stone, stood the merchant and cried out very loudly:

"For three sacks of flour and ten measures of olive oil I shall sell Miriah that is twelve, and so beautiful that I was offered a herd of camels for her by one prince, but he later died. Oho! Oho! Who will give three sacks of flour and ten measures of olive oil, for me to come back to the city, as the night is coming? All the teeth has this virgin, good sight and good hearing, and eats so little that she has to be forced to eating with a strap. She is of princely kin, and can cook pilau, as well as clean stains on silk! Don't you hear me, worthy people, or has Allah taken your wits away, if no one wants to buy a virgin for three sacks of flour and ten measures of olive oil? Would that none of you woke up tomorrow, you mangy dogs!"

The Caliph came closer and listened; the merchant, having noticed his rich attire, raised his voice even more and called out:

"Buy her, worthy Persian, so that you had comfort and joy, and progeny similar to yourself! I shall sell her very cheap to you: for six sacks of flour and twenty measures of olive oil, although I paid more her father, who is a Sultan in a faraway land."

"You demanded less for her in the first place," said the Caliph.

"I must have gone mad or my tongue dried out, and even if it were so, would I dare to offend you, demanding so little? Buy her worthy lord, don't you see how she is smiling at the sight of your face that shines as if you were a Caliph." This said, he kicked her slightly and whispered:

"Laugh, or I will tear your skin off!" But she burst with a sudden cry, which she could not contain in her chest any longer.

"What did you do to her?" called out ar Rashid.

"Watch that I don't kick you in your fat stomach, you thief!" shouted the merchant and spitting in his beard out of great anger, dragged the girl away with force, almost carrying her, for she drooped on his hands.

The Caliph looked at them, struggling to see in the dark, then he looked sadly at his ring, in which the teardrop was enclosed, and entered the bridge.

Either the day was so horrible, or Allah intended to show his servant, Rashid, all the human misery, for he only managed to make a couple of steps, when a great cry and grumble bumped into him, like someone running fast bumps into your chest suddenly. Many people, stooping, stared into murky, soaked with darkness and disease water, none of their faces terrified, but all hopelessly sad.

The Caliph came closer and like the others, looked into the water, flowing noiselessly, only sometimes babbling with hollow gurgle or an evil and angry whisper—for who is powerful and mighty does not express anger with a yell, but kills without the word instead. He noticed down below liquid gloom and sluggish darkness, crawling ahead, slimy and slippery.

"I cannot see anything!" called someone, looking into the darkness.

"I can," called the other.

"What do you see?"

"Quran floating on the water."

"Allah Bismillah!" the crowd groaned.

"Holy book cannot drown!"

"Allah Rossoulah!"

"Misery! Misery!"

And one of them that knew how things were, was explaining it to the others that came later:

"An old man flung himself off the bridge into the river. His name was Yusuf and he used to sit on the bridge, all day long. People were putting in his bowl what they could, and he, in exchange would read out the Quran and explain each sura wisely and sensibly."

"The Prophet shall reward him! Why did he take his life though?"

"For many days now, nobody has given anything to him, for we suffer great poverty and despair. What can you give out of an empty bag, O Allah!? His strength and his voice left him, and his eyes got blinded out of hunger. He managed to find his way to the water though."

"Misery!" cried everybody.

"Silence!" some voice called, "A dead man is in the vicinity and one should observe silence."

Everyone ceased talking suddenly, then only whispered, their words pale and very, very sad.

"He was a holy man," they were saying, "and knew a lot; for just two dates he would tell a tale so beautiful that no other man would come up with, and had someone been sad and poor, he would tell them for free."

Caliph Harun ar Rashid didn't hear their further words, for having covered his face with his hands, he fled this horrible place, but sorrow, fleeter than a black steed from sultan's stables, caught up with him fast and fell like a cloud on the Caliph's heart.

* * *

"O my brothers! Ten pieces of gold I need to be happy! Not more, not less, but ten pieces weighed properly, not cut craftily with a knife. O Prophet! Let the thousand people donate and give it to me, and I shall give them happiness, compared to which, sultan's treasures are worthless. Prophet told me a secret in my sleep, so that I made happy those who love him. Ooh! Ten pieces of gold I need, and I shall do more than Allah and all the sages that were and will be until the end of the world did! Who will pity and help me? On Prophet's beard! Don't walk by, and listen to my words, containing the mystery, and he who hears me shall be happy!"

Thus, whining loudly, called out from the other end of the bridge, a man strangely thin, almost translucent, his eyes burning like coals, and flying hair; his shirt undone on his chest, no turban on his head and so unlike the others that even a very hurried man, would have to stop and look at this face that spectres or terminally ill people have.

"Mad is this man," someone said and as if frightened with his own words, quickly departed. The other spoke:

"Should he stand here until kingdom come, he might collect six pieces of gold, but he shall never gather ten pieces."

Hearing these words, everybody laughed for it was easier to turn the river in opposite direction, than collect so much gold. And he, as if not hearing this laughter, rose his voice even more and called so loud that he could be heard on both sides of the river:

"Mercy! Mercy! For a few coins, joy shall rule the earth and defeated shall be the most dreadful enemy that lurks everywhere, but no one knows how to overcome it, save for Allah and myself."

"Mind," someone shouted, "that Allah doesn't punish you with death!"

"Death?!" shouted the thin man, I am not scared of death, but death is scared of me. O, brothers! God is hearing me and I swear to him that I am neither thief, who wants to steal the gold, nor cheat, for I am speaking out loud. I am the one that found happiness, one who knows where it is, but I don't have ten pieces of gold to make a golden key and enter the cave where the mystery dwells. Twelve thousand books I read and for a long time now, no sleep closed my eyes, unless by force."

Entered the crowd Harun ar Rashid and hearing all these words precisely, he could not see a speaker, for his eyes were foggy with bloody haze, and out of it, with a spooky sight, looked at him all these miserable faces, whom he beheld at close quarters on this day; he had to wipe eyes with his hand, before he caught sight of this strange man that asked for so extraordinary alms. He looked nimbly in his face, trying to spot madness in it. He could only see an immense paleness though, on which glimmered from time to time flickering sparkle of hope; stretched over the crowd, white and thin hands of this man quivered nervously, his body shivering. Then he would squint his eyes and open his mouth lightly, as if wanting to catch a breath; at this moment doubt would creep out onto his face from below his eyelids, like a grey wall, and he looked, with this suddenly deceased face, and in his tattered grey robe, as if he came out of the darkness of the night, by some mysterious means.

"It is not an ordinary man," thought Rashid and decided to listen some more to his words that rose after a while, as if with difficulty, after too short rest, and were walking over the crowd like group of exhausted people, trudging through the hot sands, faltering; soon though, as if refreshed by the night's cool, they shouted more briskly, flashed lighter and started to call loudly:

"O my brothers! I have been standing here for two years now and begging you, day in and day out, before last wayfarer passes me. Woe is me! Why didn't I drop dead in the desert or hung myself on the palm tree? What did I come to you for, carrying happiness in my both hands; for you to pass by, spitting with scorn? And from the East to the West no one experienced this immense sweetness that I am preparing, and should I fail only because of lacking ten pieces of gold, owned by any robber or olive merchant? And I shall tell you this: if need be, I shall cut my hand for this gold and take my eye out; if need be, for me to cry for every piece of gold for a hundred days. I swear to Allah that I shall do it without complaint. For great is my work, and my joy shall be greater than my mortification, my work is greater than sea or a desert, greater even than entire earth. If I told you about it, you would kiss my hands and feet, and flap of my robe."

"Oh! oh! the crowd laughed, "You are beautiful like an odalisque!"

It disconcerted him for a moment, but then, with a sudden and angry movement, he brushed his hair aside and stared at them in silence, with great contempt, ousted from his eyes only by tears; his voice broke, when he was finishing:

"...And I cannot tell you before the right time comes, for human mind might baffle... May my tears drop on you."

"Say no more!" shouted someone from the crowd and raised his staff, but then, as if he pondered that it becomes not beating a madman, he just spat in his direction and left; the others started to leave too, some laughing out lout, others pitying the man, from whom Allah taken his reason, punishing him for some severe offence. Yet another were leaving in silence, thinking in the depth of their hearts, how unattainable happiness is, if one has to pay so much gold for it.

This man, very tired, grew very surprised, when he saw someone looking him in the eyes, neither pityingly nor abusively, but as if wanting to see through to the bottom of his soul. As if enslaved by this sight, unintentionally he bowed down his head in a greeting. And Rashid asked dignifiedly:

"What is your name?"

"Athros!" answered he. "Do not wonder at my name, for I come from Egypt."

"Are you a sage?"

"I don't know, my Lord!"

"I considered seeds of wisdom in your words. Tell me then, where you acquired it from?"

The other remained silent for a while, as if recalling something with pleasure and after some time his face started to burn and eyes sparkled.

"I know a lot," he answered, "but my wisdom is out of this world."

"Who taught you things you know?"

"The dead! answered he, but with quiet whisper, as if scared that the river will hear him, for no one was on the bridge, nor in the vicinity.

"You have uttered a horrible word," Rashid told him, "aren't you scared of the night?"

"I am not scared of death!"

"You are a strange man. What dead taught you?"

"Those lying in Egyptian soil, buried in the sands, hidden in caves, or resting in the pyramids." Suddenly he became anxious. "Why are you examining me like a judge?"

The Caliph sensibly spoke to his soul for some time, than slowly enunciating his words he answered:

"I am the one who shall give you ten pieces of gold."

Like when burning torch is applied to dried flax, and the flax shoots with soaring flames, so this man stood aflame; and because these words were too unexpected, and his doubt deadly, so like a man hit suddenly in the head with a club by some strongman, reels and falls down like a palm tree cut at its base; so he reeled, and having shouted some unconceivable words, non existent in unlearned people's dictionary, dropped at the Caliph's feet and laid as if dead. Harun ar Rashid nodded his head sadly and gathered that with his words, he killed this man, for it happens often that benefaction kills equally fast as great injustice. After a moment he rejoiced though, noticing that this fallen man shook suddenly, as if the frost hit him on the back of his skull with its bony palm, and then hearing silent weeping at his feet.

At first silent sob gurgled in this man, like a pot of water, put on fire begins to gurgle until it boils, then louder and louder and so strong that all his body was shaking. Finally, his eyes flowed with great stream of hot tears, dropping on saffian sandals of Rashid and on the street dust. The Caliph felt that his heart wrings and mounts from his chest to his throat, so having stooped, he wanted to raise this man off the ground. But the other, having embraced with his both hands Harun's feet, was kissing them.

"What are you doing?" he said and stepped back.

But Athros lied motionless for another while, then rose to his knees, and kneeling, as if he were looking towards Mecca, spoke:

"I do not bless you, my Lord, for what is a blessing, compared to what I am going to pay you back for the gold?!"

"What can I obtain from you, whose clothes are in tatters?"

"My Lord," said Athros, "I am richer than Harun ar Rashid."

Having heard his name, the Caliph said:

"You were saying that you called out for help in vain here: why didn't you come to him, whose name you just mentioned? He would have given you the gold without hesitation."

"Caliph Rashid?"

"Indeed."

But Athros saddened and spoke without grief, but with his voice sad:

"No mother calls her child that went missing in the desert so long-ingly, like I, standing countless nights, by the wall of his palace, called for Rashid's help."

"I haven't heard your voice!" said the Caliph surprised; then having realized that he accidentally revealed his identity, he reddened. Athros did not comprehend the words of the noble man though, for he said:

"If you were a Caliph, you would hear me."

Hearing these words, Harun turned slightly towards the city and quickly said:

"Night is already late now and Baghdad rests in blissful sleep. You should rest too, and stop bothering: your worry is dead now."

"But you shall never die, worthy Lord," answered Athros, strangely sharply, not in the way that one says blessings.

"I do not understand you!" said the Caliph, affected with the strange sound of his voice.

"You shall understand me as early as today, before sun rises. Do you have the gold with you, or should I come for it? If so, realize that I will go to get it, even if you lived in hell or in the middle of saline swamp in the desert."

"I have it with me!" said Harun and having produced his pouch, he enumerated on stretched Athros' palm, ten pieces, shining famously, not defiled with use yet, unused and uncut. Athros shivered with all his body, only his hand, on which Harun put the gold didn't move, as if made of steel, and it seemed that no strongman could open it, when he clenched it after a while and put to his chest, in place where heart is. He stared with strange sight and spoke, his voice immensely touched:

"Realize that at the moment Allah is looking at nothing in this world but us."

"Is he rejoiced?"

"At this moment Allah is afraid," whispered the other. "Follow me, my Lord, so that you were first to see, what the world will talk about until its end."

This heard, Harun thought at first that having committed a good deed, he should bid this man that was threatening Allah amid the night and whose eyes were insane goodbye; but Athros, having noticed that the other lingered, bowed his head down and repeated:

"I am telling you that for ten pieces of gold, you have bought your luck, I beg you then, to come with me, so that I can pay off my debt."

Harun tried with invisible movement the dagger behind his belt and realizing that it easily leaves the sheath, followed him, without a word, ready for anything.

* * *

They walked for an hour or so, in great silence, unthinkingly silencing even their steps, as if they set out for precious horses stealing in the desert. They both weighed some thoughts, and Harun, raising his eyes to the sky from time to time, prayed in his soul: "I do not know what this man intends to do, so protect me, O Allah, and deign to restore his common sense, had he lost it by your inconceivable decrees."

But the sky was silent, its face black and unfathomable. The narrow and crooked streets were empty, only occasionally one could see a grimy light trickling through a chink in the wall, like a pus from a bad, purulent eye, and sometimes wistful howling of a dog, advertising death, could be heard.

Athros walked first, being able to see at night, and Harun followed him closely, unaware of their path nor whereabouts; he only remembered that the river was to his right, feeling breeze and hearing distant hum from that direction. Feeling no weariness, he was rather excited with this eerie adventure, never before experienced in his life, for never before had he strayed so far from his palace, without his servants and entourage; he had this strange feeling though that this inconspicuous man would reveal some extraordinary thing to him. Or maybe it was the night that caused the soul of Caliph Harun, until then quiet and sedate like the soul of a sage, to jerk in Harun's chest and flap its wings, and he unable to either stop it or hide, would quite often start to tremble and felt that his mouth dried.

It was strange, but Harun ar Rashid started to play with the thought that his guide lost his way in jumble of the streets and they would be walking like this until the sunrise, so he stepped back suddenly, when the other stopped in front of a stone house, remote from the others, and having bowed down low, said quietly:

"Deign to come in, my Lord!" and awkwardly started opening the gate in the wall.

Ar Rashid plucked up his courage and stepped forward, clutching in his feverish hand, pommel of a dagger, cold as a serpent's body. Athros, following him, closed the gate carefully and led him through hollow stone yard, then having opened the second doors, led him into a corridor and into a spacious chamber, lit wit three lamps. Suddenly Rashid stepped back and began to tremble, leaning against the wall.

"What is this?" he whispered.

"Fear not, my Lord!" answered Athros, "This is a dead man that shall do you no harm; you can see for yourself that he is all wrapped in shrouds and has no dagger. This is a mummy of one Egyptian sage, the most learned in the world, but still death's wisdom was bigger than his."

"Why don't you put him to rest in his grave, or throw into the river?"

"Would you do this to your father?"

At this moment, Rashid realized that this man is insane, and got terrified. And the other continued:

"This is my father that left me two thousand years ago, but knowing that I will be born one day, he hid riches for me in his grave."

"What did he leave you?"

"His brain and his heart. Do you want to see them?"

This said, he took out a small bundle out of wrought iron chest, unwrapped yellow of age, silk shawl and spread before Rashid's eyes, the papyrus scroll, very faded and very damaged.

"This is his brain and his heart; his brain knew all the things one could know in this world, and his heart was great, therefore God killed him, so that he didn't exalt himself and see the mystery, thanks to which God is God—for had he found it, then there would be no difference between a man and Allah, who is the master of mystery and kills with it like with a knife. He kissed the scrolls and then put them to his forehead, as if he thus wanted to transfer into his mind, wisdom contained therein.

"Be seated, worthy Lord, so that you could listen carefully to all I am going to tell you, for this man leaning against the wall and en-shrouded, has his mouth sealed by hateful death with seven seals, and therefore is not capable of speaking his case. Look carefully though, and you will see that when the lamp shines stronger, his face twitches and eyes laugh, out of extraordinary joy that there is someone to avenge him and that there is a benefactor that helped me to it. He greets you, through me, at my home! Please, be seated, my Lord."

Harun, in whose head some great sea was humming, and hands trembled, sat on low sofa and waited in silence, looking greedily, what was about to happen. He could see Athros coming to the fire-place, striking the fire and blowing nimbly, to bring life into the pale sparks that having reddened with fiery blood after a while, started to bite greedily dry wooden chips with their red teeth, cracking loudly; then he hung on the chain over the fire an iron pot full of some potion—and doing it all, he was whispering some eerie words:

"By the power of life and might of death... fear of a mystery, O Ptah!... seven good and seven bad forces, to make light, what is dark... to make round, what is shapeless... Look back, and you shall see death, look forward, and you shall see death... By demise of the West and power of the East, and by joy of the spring... Osiris!"

The Caliph cocked his ears for these words, but didn't dare ask about anything; he waited long, before Athros, as if reminding himself of Caliph's presence, turned to him, scrolls in his hand and having stooped over Caliph, spoke with a voice, as if each word was coming out of a grave:

"For a hundred years was this man writing that is now sleeping eternal dream there, these words; each of them contains his blood and sweat, and such suffering, of which no one knows in this world; when he was about to put down the last word, he weakened and was unable to find it, although he was looking for it for thousand nights in the darkness, using his heart as a lantern. Look here! Here is an empty space, resembling the paleness of a corpse, and further down are characters again that transliterated say: "Death is coming... May he, who shall come after me, overcome it...""

"What does it mean?" asked Rashid quietly.

Athros, as if failing to hear the question, read on, his eyes dimmed with haze:

"...Let him leave his father and mother, let him restrain from wine drinking, let him renounce everything earthly, until he finds what he has been looking for... And most of all, let him beware of a woman..."

"Aren't there any women at your home?" the Caliph interrupted him.

"Haven't you heard what the dead man said? Realize that grand thought is like a steed, and woman is like a thong that hobbles its legs. I followed his teachings and found the word, which he had failed to find!"

Rashid listened carefully.

"I knew everything then, but look here, what the sage wrote: 'You shall take ten pieces of gold according to measure I named, and having thrown it into, what you already know about, you shall pronounce three times the word that you are familiar with...' I knew it all, but I had no gold, my benefactor, whatever your name is."

"I go by the name of Mohammed," said the Caliph.

"May your name be blessed, son of righteous father! In just a while you shall know more than seven thousands sages."

This said, he approached the fire and started to stare strangely in the pot, embraced with fire from all sides like with a storm; then having raised the lid, started to slowly and carefully drop into the boiling liquid one piece of gold after another, acting with great concentration, and looking at his moving lips, one could guess that he was saying, with inaudible whisper this magic word that he was commanded to utter, by a dead man, leant against the wall.

Flames belched higher, covering Athros' face with a bloody glow, and his flying hair, painted with shine of a flame, seemed to move like snakes; his eyes were shining, widened, and stared into the fire without a wink, as if accustomed to this sight.

Rashid, having recalled Athros' words that when brought to light, the mummy's face comes to life, looked at the corpse wrapped in yellow shrouds and shivered, for its dried face seemed to be adorned with a grin, and its lively eyes shone with red glimmer; Rashid felt that his hair bristled under the turban and blood chilled in his veins so that he froze, terrified. He was pale like a canvas and could not breathe.

"It is fulfiled! said Athros finally, in a loud voice, and having approached the mummy, prostrated before it, and seemed to be praying quietly.

When he rose and stood in the lamp's circle, he looked like a man that dragged himself out of bed after a heavy illness, to see the sun, unseen for many days, and revive with a new life. Sweat, in big drops, trickled down his forehead, marking distinctly its cadaverous paleness, in which eyes burned like two torches; one could see he is very exhausted, as after immense effort, for he faltered walking. He sat heavily before the Caliph and smiled a smile, in which there was gratitude, but yet little forgotten joy, and one could see that at the moment he struggles to remember, how to form face into a joyful smile. He started to speak, his voice quiet:

"Now, I shall explain you everything Mohammed, while the potion you have gilded, cools down."

"Speak!" whispered Rashid, and listened, his head resting against the wall.

"Tell me kindly, my worthy Lord, who is the greatest enemy of a man?"

Rashid pondered for a while and said:

"Himself."

"You answered like a man that ruminated a lot and has lots of sense; although a man kills oneself not out of anger but out of pain. Don't you know who the greatest enemy of a man is?"

Thought again for a while Rashid and said tentatively:

"A woman."

"You pronounced the name of an even scarier enemy that destroys a lot and causes great torment, having poison in her soul and on her lips; although one can run away from a woman. Don't you know what the name of the enemy is, from whom one can neither run, nor hide anywhere?"

"Death!" said Rashid in timid whisper.

"Yes, death!" repeated Athros, his voice hollow and contaminated with hatred.

"Death," spake his silent voice, at which Rashid winced. Athros noticed it.

"It wasn't him," he said, pointing to the mummy with his eyes, "for he is dumb. It was echo, for one cannot pronounce this terrifying word, without it echoing amid the night."

They both remained silent, weighing thoughts as if staring at this black word that fell off their lips like an infested fruit falls off the tree.

"Here, this man," continued Athros after a while "this dead man set out to overcome death."

"Allah!" whispered Rashid.

"He got to know all that could be known, and learned the wisdom of all nations that were from the beginning of the world. This is when he found first word, having understood the mystery of water. Then, for many years, he had been researching secrets of plants, animals, and stones, and found the second word. When he put these two words together, he was looking out for the stars' trajectories and secrets of the moon, and secrets of sun at daytime and after many years he enscrolled the third word that was great and horrid. He was still young then, his hair black, but having put down this word, he also put down that having comprehended it, he went grey overnight, and madness flew past his head so close that he could feel its hot breath."

"Allah!" whispered Rashid, and the other continued:

"He realized then that he must comprehend the mystery of fire, and he discovered it one night, making a bonfire in the desert. Having written down the fourth word, he also wrote down that fear started following him since then, like a shadow, and terror so horrible that no one experienced before. O Ptah! Great is the mystery of fire.

"Living in this constant fear, he started to search for the soul of a number and he was talking to it for twelve years, filling in many scrolls, to find a way to the mystery of death, through its scary labyrinth. Finding the soul of a number, he wrote down the fifth word, and it was scarier than madness and redder than blood. Here, look... Here is written the word, whose face is evil and so beautiful that one cannot take one's eyes off it, but at the same time it cannot be stared at too long, like at a sun; as he didn't know about it, look what he wrote here: 'Having found the mystery of a number, I went blind and can see nothing, although my eyes are open.'"

Rashid glimpsed timidly at the mummy and noticed its eerie eyes, now already deceased, and a shiver went down his spine. Athros unscrolling the papyrus, continued:

"This is the sixth word and the last, denoting the mystery of earth. He comprehended it, and wrote it down, but seven words were needed."

"What was seventh word supposed to mean?"

"It was supposed to be scariest of them all, and describe the mystery of the world where the dead go. This old man used to enter tombs and wake up the dead, to talk to them, but none of them would answer him and failing to find the seventh word, he died. But I have found it!"

Harun stared at him with insane expression and held his breath.

"Did you speak to a dead man?"

"As I speak with you."

"Who with?"

"With him!" said Athros quietly, and bowed his head down with respect, having turned towards the mummy.

The Caliph trembled like a leaf during a storm, and felt that fear, greater than the one experienced by a man at the moment of his death, looks him straight in the eyes, searching for his heart; he felt its icy palm taking his heart of his chest and out into the night and darkness. "He is not a human," he though with great mind's effort, "He is a seitan."

And the other, beholding emptiness, was enunciating eerie words, each shining lighter and lighter, like an envoy that brought good news, first says great words, but clumsy, so entangled like deer with their horns, and only later, describing the victory precisely, sets his words alight with a torch and flame of memory and covers each word with sunshine, so that his and his listeners' eyes were becoming brighter.

"I am the one who overcame death. I am the one, who can grant lives, like Allah. What more can he do? It is not me who is scared, but at this very moment he is shivering before me, saying: 'O Prophet! Why didn't I kill this man before he was born?' Do you know why I devoted my life for it, knew no bliss, but only labour and pain? Have you ever seen a slave chained to a galley, together with another slave, hitting his head against a ship's side and thus killing himself, so that the other could flee, having cut the corpse's leg? I did it as vengeance, for everything that lives is in Allah's hand and trembles before him, for he is the one that sent death on earth—his slave driver, and when it cracks its whip, man dies. Akbar Allah! —he called out—send death to my home now, and I shall greet it, laughing, like a lame dog or a snake, whose fangs were pulled by my intellect."

He rose, saying these rude words and looked in the ceiling, with immense hatred on his face, but at the same time, beauty so grand that the Caliph looked at him with surprised admiration.

"Seitan!" he whispered for the second time. Athros spoke:

"In this pot there is labour of many sages, wiser than Jewish King Solomon, blood of many hearts and hatred of many souls, but there are neither hearts, nor hatred in it greater than that of mine and him, who cannot bless me, for his hands are mortally stiff. Out of this pot everyone shall drink now, and no one is going to die anymore, unless they take their life themselves. And you, Mohammed, for giving me the gold, whose red blood I needed, shall drink it first, for you to live forever."

This said, he took the pot off the chain and carrying it as carefully as if he carried his own heart, out of which blood might spill, put it on the ground and removed the lid. The haze similar to a bloody vapour rose up and spilled across the chamber the fragrance as fresh as that of spring, mountain breeze, or smell of a sea; Athros inhaled it with pleasure and whispered:

"Do you feel the scent of life?

The scent gave the Caliph a vertigo sensation, but soon his sight cleared and he felt wave of blood rushing into his heart and his entire body suddenly filled with robustness and strength. He could clearly see then, as Athros, having taken a silver mug out of a chest; poured in it several drops of horrible blood-red potion, and having stretched his hand, spoke kindly like a sultan that grants a criminal some immense favour:

"Take this and drink!"

73

The Caliph didn't move a muscle, but stared in his eyes sharply.

"Let me," he said, "tell you something, before I accept this price-less gift."

"Speak!" answered Athros and replaced the mug.

"Athros," spoke Caliph, "horrible is the thing you have done"

"I am well aware of that. Why are you wasting your words?"

"Tell me: a man in whose veins this potion flows shall live forever?"

"He will live forever... yes he will!"

"And he will praise you, as I am praising you now. Tell me though, are you the only one that knows the secret recipe, accord-ing to which this potion is brewed?"

"Two of us know it:, me, and this dead man."

"You shall not die, though?"

"You said! I shall not die".

"And he shall not rise from the dead?"

"Your question is sad; why do you hurt my heart? This man will not rise from the dead. Death and a tiger would not give back a prey."

"Is the biggest of the mysteries written on this scroll?"

"As you can see, but no one can read it. But seventh and the most important word I carved in the bark of my heart, undecipherable to no one either. Is there anything more you wish to say?"

The Caliph's face was pale, with great furrow between his brows, denoting suffering.

"I haven't told you the most important thing yet. Realize that before I met you by the bridge, I had seen a man dying of starvation. Will this potion feed a man for long life?"

"Isn't it enough for you that a man shall live as long as he pleases?"

"You shall thus cause a man to suffer, not for few years, but for a thousand?"

"It has to be like that in this world that someone suffers. Why are you worried with minor things in the face of the paramount one? Have you seen anything else that touched you? Oh!"

"I have seen suffering and faces full of pain. Then I have seen one sage fling himself into the river, not to suffer anymore. This one escaped from life."

"Although, on their knees, Harun ar Rashid and leper beggar alike, shall beg me for even a drop of this potion."

"Seitan!" the Caliph thought for the third time, but aloud he said:

"You have discovered horrific thing, Athros, and Allah shall punish you for it."

"With what? With death?"

"It can be that you shall beg on your knees that someone do you a favour and kill you."

Athros woke two lightnings in his eyes and said threateningly:

"You gave me ten pieces of gold, and I return it to you, a millionfold. What more do you want?"

"I want you to tell me, whether people living longer, will suffer less?"

"I do not know!"

"I am telling you, they shall suffer a hundredfold, and death won't come to their rescue. And I am also telling you that grievous crime is what you committed."

"Begone!" shouted Athros.

Harun leant over him, deadly pale, his right hand clasping firmly the dagger's pommel, and spoke with a voice cold and sharp as a knife:

"I am telling you that no one shall drink your potion."

At the sound of his voice, Athos shivered.

"Begone! Who are you? What? Begone! Begone!

At this moment, Harun ar Rashid, with a move swift as a thought, plunged the dagger into Athros' heart, before the other managed to catch the movement with his eyes; he just spread his hands, spat out of his mouth some word that fell dumb the very same moment, for the blood drowned it, and having twitched in horrible spasm, lumped down to the ground.

Harun ar Rashid stood pale, bloodied knife in his hand and panted heavily; after a while he shivered of cold, flung the dagger away and awfully quiet, gripped the iron pot with his hands and spilled all the liquid, which flowed with a red stream over the ground. Then he took the scroll and having approached the fire, he burned it slowly and long, until the last piece smouldered.

At this moment he heard the voice, so horrid that his soul froze; icy terror gripped his head with its hands and turned it, so that Harun ar Rashid could see a mummy leaning against the wall, slid down and crumbled to dust. The Caliph was fleeing; and passing the corpse of Athros, thought for the fourth time:

"It was an evil and dreadful spirit. I have killed the seitan."

And he came out into the air, already swarmed with first sunrays. He closed the gate with care and headed down the hum-filled streets, and the farther he was from this spooky house, the lighter his soul felt, and when he stood in the courtyard of his palace, he was radiant like a sun. Having noticed by the fountain, eunuchs sprinkling water, trying to bring round the virgins he had given to the envoys of Charlemagne, for they swooned out of excessive weariness, he ordered to send them fresh ones, for immensely kind was Caliph Harun ar Rashid, called the Just, this day.

Hassan and His Five Wives

Abd ul Moshed sat in a shabby café, drinking coffee out of a dirty cup; and whenever a smile crossed his face, the honorable man would raise his hand slowly and nobly, and stroke a silvery beard, a man's pride. Then he was thinking deeply why the porter, his veins swollen on his temples, carries the huge sack on his back, and not himself—being stronger than three porters? And Abd ul Moshed smiled again, continued stroking his beard, very content, understanding that Allah divided everything between the people justly and accurately, for if everybody were well, no-one would pray for fortune's turn. He also thought that he's carrying a heavy burden too, namely his great intellect that doesn't let him sleep, often waking him up in the middle of the night demanding:

"Abd ul Moshed! Wake up and think why there exist dromedaries with only one hunch, while there are also camels having two?"

He would then wallow in his bed until the crack of dawn, ruminating mightily and cursing his district-famous, rabble-admired, great mind, for usually towards evening some cobbler or even a baker would come round, and having salaamed him, would whine these words:

"You are as wise, Abd ul Moshed, as this camel, that knowing no road in the desert will get to the oasis after all; solicit me then, for sorrow troubles my heart!" Then would answer the noble man:

"Tell me everything; for it is not your fault that God created you a fool—and a cobbler, to add insult to injury."

And Abd ul Moshed wasn't swaggering at all, but he would listen to the grumbles patiently and long; his eyes squinted, not so carelessly though, not to watch if the poor man steals his shoes or a cup encrusted with golden veins, in his perplexity. Having listened, he would say:

"Your worry comes from thinking of it. You are a cobbler, but misfortune is not a saffian shoe for you to look at, all day long. Go now, and going back home laugh out loud, so that everybody can hear it, and shouldn't it help, come back tomorrow."

The cobbler would then run down the streets, laughing, so that the people were running out of their houses and dogs escaped, howling. On the next day he would come back sad, complaining that it hadn't helped, and so it continued for many days, until kawas[*], having grabbed him firmly by the collar, led him to a madhouse. That's where he realized he was indeed a lucky man, and that all his sorrows were caused by his wife who was a shrew. And blessed the cobbler his benefactor.

Regretfully Abd ul Moshed's fame grew because of this, and he was worried with the great fame, causing him many concerns, so he used to say that fame is like a bad woman that keeps babbling over the ear, and will not let you sleep even in your grave.

At the moment though, he was feeling immense bliss, as if he were at the baths, and just started to speculate why flies can walk on the ceiling, and humans cannot—when stood in front of him his great friend Hassan—a hot-headed man and unable to ponder.

---

[*] here - policeman.

He was very fretful and panted heavily, so he only managed to utter these words:

"Allah is the greatest!" Beholding him quietly, Abd ul Moshed said:

"Haven't you found out anything newer?" Hassan wondered on these words, and having sat on his legs, waggled for some time, before he started to speak.

"I have been looking for you, Moshed, first at home..."

"One is not at home all the time..." Moshed interrupted him.

"You have truly said, but then I have been looking for you at the baths, then bazaar and a mosque, and I couldn't find you anywhere..."

Smiled pitifully wise Abd ul Moshed and said graciously:

"Had Allah equipped you with some wits, you would have immediately come to the conclusion, not going anywhere that if I am at a café, then I am neither at home nor at baths, mosque, nor bazaar, and you would have met me here."

First amazed, then with immense esteem, hot-headed Hassan beheld him, and clucked in admiration, while Moshed shut his eyes for a while, very content with his wisdom. Then he asked:

"What hurried you so much Hassan, Mustafa's son, without consideration that he, who is on a hurry is always late?" Hassan wrung his hands and having lowered his voice, whispered:

"I came to you for an advice, O Wisest, for I have suffered a horrible misfortune."

"Misfortune is never horrible if it can be helped," said Moshed, "but tell me what has happened to you? Has your horse died, or your donkey been stolen?"

His friend looked around to see if no-one was listening, then he spake:

"My misfortune is not that big, but almost equally dire. One of my wives has been unfaithful to me, and I don't know which one!" Moshed looked at him pitifully, nodded his head eminently, smiled nine times, then stroked his beard.

"Have you ever had a toothache, Hassan?" he asked.

"Why do you ask me such an odd question? Yes I have."

"Wasn't it all the same to you, which one was aching?"

"Indeed, but what has one to do with another?" He started to rage thinking that wise Abd ul Moshed mocks him; the latter mused deeply though, and asked:

"How did you know of this?"

"I saw," answered Hassan, "a young man exit my wives chambers, who having noticed me started to run away."

"That's too bad!" Hassan looked at him anxiously. Abd ul Moshed continued, "Had he grabbed you by the beard and hit you on the head or called you thief and a cheat, that would mean your wives are old and toothless, and he didn't get lucky with them, but his escape means he wants to come back."

"Misery! Misery!" groaned Hassan.

"How many wives do you have, Mustafa's son?"

"Five only, for last year was hard, and three of my camels died of disease."

"How often do you beat your wives?"

"Once a day only, for I don't have much time—do I do wrong, Abd ul Moshed?

"I haven't said that, but I reckon it is better rarely and more severely than often and leniently, for when they get accustomed to it, they don't think much of a bamboo, which causes them to put on weight and makes them prone to bad things.

"Oh! oh!" wailed Hassan.

"Tell me one more thing. Did you tell them when you were going to be back, leaving home that day?"

"Yes, I said I was going to be back in a little while, I did it on purpose, for them to be afraid."

Smiled genially, old Abd ul Moshed, and said sweetly:

"Friend of mine, you are just as stupid as a lame ostrich. Don't you know that woman understands speech inversely and there is only one cure for her slyness: always tell her the truth, for she will fail to recognize it and trying to translate it into her language, she will fall into the trap. It's a dangerous way though, for failing to understand the trick, she might easily go crazy and lose her mind. You have done the very wrong thing, brother Hassan, and what do you want from me now? To find you a culprit? Am I a kawas, am I a kadi?* Do I know everything anyway? I know that ram is a ram and me is me, but do I know what's underground or at the bottom of the sea? Do I know what is inside woman and why she betrayed you?"

"You know everything! said Hassan.

"Well that is not true. There was a great scholar in Baghdad, who had two wives only; he knew how many stars there are in the sky, and when it would rain; he knew how the cure of plague. So wise was the man that the Caliph gave him an old horse once; yet this great man died of worry, for he couldn't understand why one of his wives to whom he was mean, was kissing his feet, and the other to whom he was good, when she was dying, told him that she could still live and she's only dying to annoy him. Do you hear me Hassan, Mustafa's son?

Hassan wondered greatly, and started to waggle violently, which made his misfortune look even worse; he was looking lovingly at the noble sage, wanting to melt his heart and receive his advice. Moshed melted finally, for he was of a soft heart, as any man happy that his friend and not him has just been touched by misfortune, and for that reason, great compassion filled his heart with rosy water

---

* judge.

"My friend! he finally sweetly spake, do what that Baghdad sage did—go hang yourself.

Hassan beheld him as through a fog, his beard starting to shake, his chest blown out like a sail, for he started to weep bitterly, his tears trickling down his beard, like crystal dewdrops trickling down the silk of a rose. And whenever the lone tear dropped from Hassan's beard, Abd ul Moshed would think: "Teardrop eats away at the rock, how on earth may my heart remain intact?" Out loud though, he uttered with great reproach, a sentence as deep as if taken out of the Quran:

"A man should never cry, unless there is good reason for it."

Hassan winced, as a man shaken by the death, or like a whirling dervish, thrown up by a devout epilepsy, raised his tearful eyes to the sky, looking to the side like a chicken looking out for a hawk, and said quietly, but extremely sadly:

"Beware that Allah doesn't punish you, for you ridicule me mercilessly. Isn't that the reason that I was betrayed by my wife, maybe the one that I called blooming lily, fed her dates, as to a noble mare, whom I would often, having kindly held her chin, fondle with most beautiful words, until she would start to sigh heavily out of pleasure? Is this not enough yet for you, Abd ul Moshed, who has a mind greater than the others, but no heart, and is callous like an eunuch?"

And rapidly, as if he had lost his mind, he jumped off his seat, and having grasped with both hands the scrawny strapper that served the coffee and hookah coals, he started to bang his head against the nearby wall and he would have damaged the wall, for the good servant's head was strangely hard and angular; but his rage suddenly weakened, he reeled back to his old place, sat on his legs and only managed to utter these words:

"I'm relieved!" he said, and came to a standstill.

The strapper, his head and honour severely damaged, started to yell frighteningly, as if he had swallowed hot coal, and started to curse Hassan, not directly though, as a vulgar person would have done, but circling around him; he first cursed the memory of the mother of his mother, then the father of his father and down to the seventh generation; then, using sonorous words, he wished his sisters leprosy, and smallpox his brothers, and uncles; all the further kin, he wished from the depth of his heart, broken arms and legs. Then, having finally slain the entire family, he addressed Hassan, Mustafa's son, directly:

"Would that you lost all your teeth and let your skin flake, let your left eye flow out, and let your wife beat out your right eye. Would that you were dying for as many years as a cripple needs to walk from here to Mecca, and let all your food change into camel's dung, you malefactor and scoundrel, you mangy dog, son of Mustafa, who was a swain that conceived a jackal. O! O! O!"

"It seems to me that this man is ill-disposed towards you!" noticed Abd ul Moshed, listening carefully. "I wish you well though, and feel for you, so I'm going to go with you, to find a culprit between your wives."

Hassan revived and his eyes started to twitch out of joy, he jumped up rapidly, to satisfy his revenge, sweeter than the sweetest delicacies, and he was ready to go. Abd ul Moshed reluctantly noticed the rush, so he thought it right to say:

"Justice is like a crippled person, so she is not in a hurry; wears a charshaf, so it cannot run as fast as a startled donkey; carries a heavy sword, which impedes the rush. Why are you hurrying then? Have you ever seen a sick man rushing to his funeral, or a ram anxious to get to the butcher? When shall you, good Hassan, learn the art of living?"

Calmed down, Hassan, Mustafa's son was, but only on the surface, for on the inside he was as hot as a pilau, celestial cuisine made of fusty rice and a dead hen, his soul troubled, like a man that is just about to swear in front of the kadi that he had never stolen anything. He therefore waited impatiently and watched Abd ul Moshed rise slowly, with dignity, although unwillingly, then search long and hard, and having produced genuine coin, said to the café owner:

"Here is your pay, but examine it carefully, for it seems to me the coin is forged." The café owner looked quickly, and knowing that Abd ul Moshed is never wrong, said just in case:

"Indeed—I do not like the coin, give me another one." Then Abd ul Moshed started to search long and hard again and handed him another coin, this one outright forged, but the café owner would swear that he hadn't seen a more genuine one in his entire life. Then Abd ul Moshed commented on this:

"You are the owner of a café and woman is a forged coin. And now bring round my donkey; you will recognize him by the white coat, and if there are two white donkeys behind the building, then mine will be the one very thoughtful, eating somebody else's fodder, having repelled his comrades. Wise is the animal, for it has been carrying me for twenty years now and we have thought many things over together."

Hassan did rush out and brought round a white, dignified beast with torn down harness, for great people and great donkeys have this feature in common that they don't care about clothing. Donkey, having noticed his master, hee-hawed frighteningly and kicked several times in the air, as if a token of great joy and proof of willingness to give his life for him. Marvelled very much Hassan and started to walk beside the donkey, already mounted by Abd ul Moshed, his legs almost touching the ground, very thoughtful.

"Stop!" he called out suddenly, "Abd ul Moshed, your donkey is going in the opposite direction, make him turn towards my house." Abd ul Moshed awoke from his musings and said reluctantly:

"It cannot be another way. My donkey has been carrying me from my home to this café, and from the café back home for twenty years and at no price will he go in another direction; therefore I shall ride to my doorstep, I will turn the donkey there and then I will be able to easily proceed to your place."

Hassan fell into despair and started to jerk the beard out of his face, wishing the beast infamous death, but he couldn't help it, so he tearfully asked Abd ul Moshed to rush the donkey with his heels to a faster pace. At this very moment though, the donkey stopped suddenly in the middle of the road and having lowered his ears, he stood stock-still.

"Bismillah!" groaned Hassan, "What happened to him?" Abd ul Moshed opened his eyes, so sweetly closed a moment ago, and said:

"He either reminded himself of something, and in a moment he will move as fast as a wind, or in the doors of nearby bakery stands the baker whose view my donkey can't bear. There, stands the bad man on the doorstep, cry out at him to hide."

Hassan picked up a stone from the ground and shouted loudly:

"Hide, you son of the swain, or I will smash your head with a stone. The noble animal can't bear the sight of your filthy face, for it's wise and hates the thief that cheats on weight of flour."

At the moment the baker disappeared in the cave of the door, like an oatcake disappears in an abyss of wide-opened gob of a ravenous warrior, Abd ul Moshed smiled, and thus spake:

"You have done the right deed and I bid you thanks, for calling my donkey a noble animal; I think that he seems to be looking at you with less contempt than before and walks faster. Now pray to Allah so that the dusk doesn't fall and that the muezzin doesn't chant from the minaret, for the donkey will stop again, as he developed a passion for chanting and likes listening to it attentively.

It was far from evening though, so no imminent bother for luckless Hassan, conspired against by two donkeys: fate and the donkey of Abd ul Moshed. So he toddled in silence, staring at the white beast as if it was a ghost, wishing him thousand diseases, but craftily and dubiously he clucked from time to time, as if he wondered at the great mind of the animal and praised it out loud.

At the same time he was meditating on his horrible misfortune, and his anger was hurrying him forward, like a noisy cowherd in a red turban hurries a lazy ox with his whip; and whenever he thought of one of his five wives' disgraceful betrayal, he would jump suddenly like a sleepy kawas that had suddenly noticed in the distance a murderer of twenty-six women and forty-seven children and starts chasing him, panting heavily; he ran forward and out-paced both sages, one mounted on the other, before he was turned back by the dignified voice of Abd ul Moshed crying:

"Come back, Hassan, for you have lost your shoe!"

The latter would come back panting like a dog that lost scent on the wind, and very tired of his wrath, started to whine and wail over his fate; then he addressed the sage with great bitterness:

"Can this be, Moshed that there are no faithful wives in this world?"

"Ask my donkey about it," answered Moshed, "I know as much about it as him."

"Your opinion could give me some consolation though..."

Abd ul Moshed mused deeply on the answer, which he was used to doing always, even when asked what his name was, in order not to say anything too lightly, then he spoke:

"There are faithful wives in this world."

"Ooh!" clucked Hassan like a dervish that beheld the heavens, or like a convict, receiving the last lash. "Ooh! But how to find them?" Moshed beheld him mercifully from the heights of his donkey and spake:

"Could you find a poppy seed in seashore sand?"

"Eh?" marvelled Hassan.

"It's similarly difficult to find such pearl between the women. That's the way it is," continued Moshed, looking in the sky. "One was punished by Allah by eye disease, another by scabies, yet another one by tooth or heart disease—all divided between them justly and bearably, but if Allah was dead set against someone, he gave him great health and five wives, as in your case Hassan. Why weren't you honest and devout? Why didn't you go to Mecca, handful of dates in your pocket? One holy man was telling me once that he had had twelve wives and his life had been very hard, so he had decided to appease God and go on a pilgrimage every year; whenever he came back, he would find one wife missing, for each time one of them would die. Now, this is how Allah had rewarded the god-fearing man, who was later sainted, for out of superhuman glee he lost his mind, and for that reason earned great respect from the people.

"I am telling you again though that there are good women on this earth, faithful and very respectable; these are ashamed of their virtue, thinking strangely that they will be ridiculed, for trying to stand out. Out of these, some make disreputable faces, while being virtuous in secrecy, and the others—like sheep that all go into the water just because two of them got into the water first—want to become unfaithful as soon as possible. For a woman is not proud of being different from all the other women; but she starts feeling immensely proud when she is like the others. It is a very peculiar and deep thing, of which you know nothing, for you are bit dim-witted and have never thought about it much. I could yet tell you lots about it, but my donkey is beginning to fret, smelling home. We are close now, I can recognize it by a little fusty smell, for not so long ago, Hassan, I dropped a dead cat into a water tank to discourage myself from drinking water. Don't you think it's a good idea, although I know that will be hard for you to understand, because of your sheer greediness?"

* * *

Night it was, when Abd ul Moshed, mounting his white rational donkey, proceeded to Hassan's house, the latter walking beside, very thoughtful. Twice had the wise man to ask the question, before the latter awoke from the painful musings.

"Commoners and animals," carried on Moshed, "have the ability to foresee the coming weather, so how do you reckon Hassan— is it going to be a fine day tomorrow?"

Hassan looked in the sky and saw a thousand stars on great, pitch-black Allah's cloak.

"I reckon it's going to be a clear day. Why do you ask?"

"I want Allah to see me," said Moshed, "Making justice in his name, he wouldn't be able to see it through the clouds."

They later walked for a long time, in great silence, and one could see that Moshed was musing over something, apparently difficult to resolve, for he had even closed his eyes—an opportunity taken advantage of by Hassan, who secretly kicked the white donkey, trying to force him to a faster pace. He soon understood though that nothing was going to persuade the noble animal, so he walked on, ready for everything; only when he recognized that his house was close, he whispered:

"Abd ul Moshed, stop thinking and look ahead, or you will bump your head against the gate, which is low."

Moshed stooped quickly and became small, while Hassan rushed to open the gate and stood by it with great respect, as if the Caliph himself was riding in his house on a white steed, fed with gourmet dates. When he rode in the yard, Hassan helped him off the donkey, which Moshed tied to a post, and having secretly whispered him several words, said:

"Lead me into your house, Hassan!"

"Be greeted in it!" said the latter and ushered the noble guest into the chamber, in which a lamp hanging from the ceiling was breathing heavily like a dying oil merchant, and smelt not so badly as one could reckon at first. Moshed set hand to his forehead, squinting across the chamber, and spake, as becomes visitor that enters his friend's home:

"Peace be upon this home that is Aladdin's palace and a Sesame, but is too small though to contain all the luck I wish upon it. Where is the sofa in this sanctuary of pleasure, Hassan?"

He was just about to answer, when by a lucky coincidence a huge spider fell into the lamp's fire that having grabbed him greedily, burst with sudden flame, like a man that ate a lot bursts with sudden joy. With the extra shine Moshed noticed a sofa by the wall, so he nobly advanced toward, and equally nobly sat on it. Then he continued:

"Your face is like the sun, friend of mine Hassan, therefore your lamp seems to be dark in comparison."

"My slaves are gluttons and keep stealing oil out of it," answered Hassan. "I will have more lamps lit, if you demand so, although I have no oil at home and would have to send for it as far as across the bridge, where it is of worst quality and produces bad odour."

Smiled kindly Moshed, knowing what a great thief his friend was, and said generously:

"Do you reckon that justice doesn't shine?"

"Indeed," answered Hassan, "Justice shines like a hundred lamps."

"So we can see the truth even at this light. Lead me to your wives, Hassan." The latter scratched his head and said:

"I wouldn't dare to lead you to their chambers Moshed, for the chambers are very airless because of endless sighs, heaved from the women's breasts, sometimes out of sadness, and often without good reason, so I will bring them here, in front of you. Before that though, I would like to ask you not to refuse a meal in my home."

Having said that, he clapped his hands and had his slave bring jam, coffee and hookah, loudly demanding that all is of the best quality, for his guest was the most respectable that had ever visited his house. Then he sat in front of Moshed and looked in his face humbly and respectfully, and when a slave brought these grand things on a big tray, he served Moshed himself.

Abd ul Moshed, with dignity, scooped jam with his fingers and raised it to his mouth with such agility that very little hanged down his fingers and dropped on the waistcoat; and then, having carefully licked his fingers, washed it down with black coffee, greatly indulging in it, and after a while a great cloud of smoke surrounded him, so he was sitting as Allah sits in the midst of the cloud, and Hassan at his feet like his Prophet. Many sweet moments passed, before Moshed, having withdrawn the hookah tip from his mouth, started to speak:

"Great is your hospitality, Hassan, and indeed Caliph Al Mahar wouldn't entertain me better, for heaven's bliss is not as sweet as your jam; coffee that I have been served reminds me of morning dewdrops on a rose, and a baby withdraws its mouth from the mother's breast with less sorrow than I have withdrawn your hookah from my mouth."

"You are embarrassing me, Moshed," interrupted Hassan. But Moshed continued:

"Would that Allah gave you great fortune, good health and strength added to that, so that you could effortlessly knock out all your servant's teeth, who instead of jam serves oil and many other unclean things; adds his facial hair to the coffee, and stuffs the hookah with camel's manure that bites the tongue and dries all saliva out of the mouth. Tell him that it was said by Abd ul Moshed, who forgives a lot. Now, have your wives summoned.

Long before that has Hassan turned his face away, now as fast as he could he summoned the servant and demanded:

"Bring my wives round here, so that I can find a culprit!"

They waited for a while, then having heard a great cry nearby, they realized that the master's voice was heard. Moshed waited quietly, but Hassan showed severe anxiety and not knowing what to do, he jerked his beard, for his soul sat on coals, although he was resting on a comfortable cushion. He acted like this for some time, for only after a long while the door opened with a great creak and five women entered the chamber, their faces veiled, for an outsider was at home. Together with them entered two eunuchs, very tall, both their faces swollen; one of them was White, his hands so long that they reached his knees, the other one was Black with a squint, his tongue cut from his mouth, which raised his price substantially. The women bowed low in front of Moshed, and the eunuchs prostrated in turns, being unable to do it at the same time for the lack of space.

"Here are my wives, Moshed!" said Hassan.

"You never say anything new," answered the former for the second time this day, and started to stare at them carefully, wanting to read their eyes, for it's known that human soul inhabits the eyes. It was too dark for him to see anything, so he was only pretending to see a lot, and whispered to himself, as if marvelling. Hassan stared at him, then again he moved his sight to his wives all standing in line, perplexed, looking with awe at the venerable man whose eyes were wise, and beard white, a token of even greater wisdom. For a long while he remained silent, as if weighing words, in order not to say anything too lightly or unwisely; stroked his beard and closed his eyes, then he nodded his head like a man that pities someone very much, then he nodded again, which is very helpful, if one searches his thoughts or wants to lift a heavy burden off his heart. There was a big silence, when Abd al Moshed, his eyes opened, finally spake:

"All indecency shall be punished, razed, and thrown into the fire!" Having said that he started musing again, and they were looking at him respectfully, silently considering the words uttered by him, out of the depth of his soul and out of his great mind's effort.

He though, of what nobody knew, tricked them with these words, and prepared for the leap like a tiger, for at the least expected moment, he said loudly:

"One of you has been unfaithful to Hassan, and I know which one!"

"Woe is me!" the White eunuch chanted in thin voice, and Black—his tongue cut out of his mouth, howled somehow strangely and hit his thighs with his hands.

"Kismet!"* groaned Hassan.

Moshed having uttered these words, beheld the women with the lightning of his eye, wanting to see which one of them winced. He would have easily recognized the guilty then, all planned beforehand in his grand mind. But they kept standing motionless, as logs of scented wood and none of them moved.

Wondered at first, Abd ul Moshed then smiled graciously like a man wanting to let everybody know he means no harm to anyone. Only Allah could see though that Moshed, with this smile, covered the embarrassment about his failed craftiness. He felt he wouldn't catch them in the net this way and wouldn't find amongst the five, the one that committed the horrible betrayal. So he mused deeply and started the descent to the bottom of his mind, finding many counsels along the way; though none of these seemed good enough. He closed his eyes and leant his head backwards; then stayed immobile and dignified like a grand judge handling a difficult case. "Allah Kerim!" thought Hassan, "The man fell asleep."

---

* fate, destiny.

Only by the movement of his lips could one recognize that Abd ul Moshed wasn't asleep, but spoke to the soul—the wisest he had ever known. He sighed then, deeply and strangely lovingly, like a not entirely unprincipled cannibal that is just about to eat his last son; stroked his beard and nodded his head movingly, at which Hassan stared with fear, and his wives with interest, as if they watched a man who, being aware of unbelievable black arts, can swallow daggers, walk on swords or lay ostrich eggs. They winced though, having heard his voice that so tender before, now hummed like a thunder, then gathering power, finally reminded them of the peal of a wagon dashing along a stony road, with mule startled and driver drunk.

"Hassan! he said, "Tell me the names of your wives. Sometimes a name can tell you a lot, and I would like to know everything, while not wishing to hurt anyone."

Hassan stepped forward and looking around his women, recognized each of them with his adept eye, one by the red hands, another by too exuberant breasts, and yet another by her being scrawny like a dervish that swore not to eat. He called each with just and rightful name:

"Here is Maisa, also called Rose Scent; I bought her for her beautiful voice, although her left shoulder blade is positioned higher than the right one. The other one, right beside her, goes by the name of Zoe, also called Pleasure Dough, for her father was a baker and her eyes squint towards the middle."

"If a woman squints," Abd ul Moshed interrupted him, "It's better if she looks towards the middle, instead of notoriously looking sideways. Who is the third one though, whose charshaf doesn't stick to the face?"

"This is Anoe, a carpet merchant's daughter that cannot wear her charshaf properly, for her nose is shapeless and resembles a hill; the fourth is called Fatima, who doesn't have any visible marks, but should the necessity arise, I will explain to you, Abd ul Moshed, how to recognize her, having undressed her. Fifth of them, the one panting heavily, due to obesity, her breasts reminding of wealth and abundance, is the daughter of a butcher, living by the grand bridge. She goes by the name of Anaziba, which also means Morning Breeze. I named them all for you Moshed, judge them now."

"You said, Hassan!" Abd ul Moshed thought for a while, then said:

"I have never done any harm to a living creature and I didn't have a heart to kill a flea that drunk my blood, so I don't want to be cruel and therefore ask that the one of you that is immensely guilty of committing adultery, sharing pleasures belonging to her master, Hassan with the others, come forward. If she pleads guilty, I promise her clemency and that apart from beheading, nothing wrong happens to her. Oh!"

Having uttered these words, he looked diligently, wanting to see, which one of them winces with fear, realizing her crime was revealed, but they stood motionless. One could only hear Hassan's heavy breath, and Morning Breeze wheezing like a samum blowing in the desert. Paled, Moshed said:

"You told me Hassan that they have crooked shoulder blades and hilly noses. Why haven't you told me that all your wives are mute?"

"Woe is me!" groaned Hassan. "Let the plague stifle them!"

Having said that he spat in his hand thrice and lost his spirit; but wise Moshed flew into a passion for an instant only, then he squinted his eyes again while with his soul's eyes he was looking for the way to these infidel hearts, cunning as a camel that his nostrils widened, tries to smell his way to the water among sands, or a moon that's stalking through the clouds, or like a calumny that craftily wandering on, among people's ears, finely bites the addressee's heart. After a while he was serene again as a faithful that had just gone past the edge of a sword lying over the abyss, dividing heaven from earth; and started to speak, his voice quiet:

"You are all pure hearted, good women, so I am ashamed of myself that trying to please your master I have put you to the test, not even thinking how much serious harm I could have caused you." At this point he winked meaningfully to Hassan; the latter's mouth opened widely in surprise and looking like a man, whose reason had been stirred by Allah's finger. Then he continued:

"The calumny has been thrown upon you by an unclean dog; would that he was dying long. Here, your master and myself have caught a young man (would that the scabies never let him sleep!) that was supposedly fleeing your chambers. We noosed him with his own turban, in which there was many unclean vermin, and having tied him to the pole we asked what he was doing in this house. He told us: 'I wanted to see Hassan's wives!'"

"Kismet!" whispered Hassan, and his wives started listening carefully. Moshed continued:

"I then asked him kindly whether he won love of any of you and whether any of you let him into her bed, disgracefully betraying her master; and this is what he answered: 'You claim to be wise, Moshed, while you don't even know that only a blind man could cherish them. For, can you cherish dromedaries (he continued) or other unclean creatures? If all Hassan's wives stood in front of me, I wouldn't even touch any of them, for can a man with a good sight, hug Fatima with crooked hips, or Maisa, who has one shoulder blade higher than the other, or maybe Anoe, whose nose resembles a hump; or should he maybe cherish Zoe, who squints like a thief or a jackal? Or maybe Anaziba, who's bloated as a mosque and pants so hard, she could propel a thousand boats?'"

Wise Abd ul Moshed hadn't even finished to speak, when the five women fell onto him and jerking hair out of their heads, started the cry so horrible that one cannot hear the like, even in hell. The shout was so immense and so unexpected that Moshed lurched, and looking at them insanely, was moving his head back. And they, wailing, shouted:

"Bastard! He swore me love! Would that his eyes leaked out!" Then they fell on the ground and rending it with their fingers, howled, as if it wasn't a lamp hanging from the ceiling, but a moon attached to a rusty chain. And they cried:

"He has seen me naked and dares say my hips are crooked! Oo!... Oo!" And the other:

"Have him killed Sir, for I was his. He told me he had never seen more beautiful woman."

Abd ul Moshed scarcely raised from the cushions, his eyes widely opened, stood petrified, then having caught his breath, he roared wildly as a lion caught in a trap:

"Hassan! They all betrayed you!"

Then having grabbed his robes with both hands, he jumped like a deer towards the door, shouting incomprehensible words in an inhuman voice, his white donkey, having seen his oddly-looking master, hee-hawed scarily and when Moshed dropped on his back, he kicked frightfully and hee-hawing all the time, he started to gallop down the silent streets.

And Hassan started to look around the chamber, and having comprehended after a while his immeasurable misery, caused by his own curiosity and the immense wisdom of Moshed, he started to slowly untie a turban from his head.

"Kismet!" he groaned silently, and shuffled away to hang himself on an untied turban.

Hang tight, good Hassan!

Sage from Overseas

Wrote the great Caliph Al Mahar, to the great ruler of India:

"There is one God, but many miserable, my brother, whose breath is scent of flowers, and each thought is a lightning, whose steed is proud to be carrying the ornament of this earth, and before whom camels kneel, understanding they will carry the sun on their back. Greetings to you a hundredfold and praise to you Sultan, who is for your people, sun at daytime, moon at night, and silvery star at dusk. Would that each of your thirty-eight sons conceived equal number, so that in thousand years time, when age bends you slightly to the ground, you would have comfort for your heart, joy for the eyes, and great pride for your soul; and I tell this to your wives that they are happy like houris, when the Prophet, strolling in paradise, deigns to gaze at them with his kind eye, for you behold them. Would that none of them were touched by the dark power of old age that pulls out teeth, wrinkles the skin and showers desert salt onto hair making them white, and would that you experienced bliss with them, as many times as countless are days in an eternity.

"Sultan, my brother! If having read my letter you go out to the seashore, you will be surprised that it's so swollen and reaches your feet, shoed with golden sandals; realize then, that it's my tears causing the sea to rise so excessively, for sitting ashore I've been crying for as long and bitterly as even the most miserable fisherman in my country doesn't. My heart is like a golden goblet, tarnished with poison; my lips are parched and wounded from bitter and painful words I speak; and my eyes are like two water tanks in a Libyan desert, without a drop of water, for I have already shed all my tears into the sea. I tell this only to you, for I know that you are of great soul and you shall understand my immense sorrow, inconceivable to myself, for I don't know where it came from and when to my palace in which there's many people and even more riches, but there is no joy, as in a house haunted by disease.

"Birds inhabit the air, fish the sea, and sorrow inhabits my soul, eating heart—the sweetest delicacy, and drinking blood—the kindest potion, and my soul, my brother, is like an immense desert, and my sorrow is like water, soaking in the sand. More and more of it subsides into the deep, pushing inside, from where it will be brought to light by no sun that delights in stroking the roses with its golden hands or lies to rest on quiet sea waters at noon, but doesn't soil its hands in the mud nor creeps into the caves, in which sleeps the black, three-headed camel of sorrow.

"Therefore I don't take my misfortune out into the sunlight, like a leper hiding in the forest or in a mountain cave, not to blind the sun's eyes, and so that no one among the living could see me, for he could kill me with a spear, shouting: 'You cannot bring happiness to your subjects, because you don't know it yourself.' Another one could come and kill me with the blow of a curved sabre, saying: 'You are too miserable to live!' And yet another could shoot me with a bow, cursing: 'Your eyes cast shadow on my field and my wheatears can't grow in the darkness.'

"Oh my brother; mightiest sultan! I don't know what death looks like in your country. In mine, in the daytime it's similar to a great darkness that fell on my chest and eyes, and at night is like a fire burning inside me, around me, everywhere. Did you manage to comprehend great wizardry of death that having abandoned one of its forms, puts on another one, but never comes as a warrior that on a black horse, curved sabre raised above his head and dagger in his mouth, dashes ahead in the cloud of dust? Why doesn't it act like that? For the brave man wouldn't be frightened by such death, holding a sword in his hand, but what happens is that a magnificent tiger runs from a stinging wasp, and a lion trembles at the sight of a mouse like a woman.

"How not to be frightened by the ghost that has neither face, nor eyes, nor hands, and at the same time a thousand faces, eyes, and hands? I am telling you: could Allah read my letter to you, he would pity me and cry, or send out angel Gabriel, saying: 'Go to the city, in which Caliph Al Mahar grieves, and dry his eyes with a silk shawl, then give him hashish of oblivion and sing in his palace all through the night, so that this man smiled, whom I have harmed.'

"But Allah won't see the content of this letter, for I will send it under guard to the borders of my country, and farther on where your Allah rules, which knows neither my affairs, nor my name. I don't want Allah's help though, for it would have to be his shame, and it cannot be that a slave embarrasses his master, or a child its father, and that great blush of aurora would sweep the face of my God, could he see what injustice he inflicted on me. Therefore I have decided to reason to the bottom of my sorrow and find a remedy for this infirmity, joy to dry tears, and I want to find what weapon to use to kill the spook that poises at the ceiling of a thousand three-hundred and forty of my chambers.

"Twelve moons have died since I intended this, and my people are wondering why there is a furrow on my forehead, as if from the sword cut, not knowing it was carved by many, many nights, as in a stone but noiselessly. They also wonder how I ,who before sunset, used to consume many courses with willing heart and joyful soul, now overcome by strange grief, only manage to swallow no more than two young lambs, skilfully toasted on coals, and chicken of petite posture that in its greasiness bathes among white rice. How could I think of my body, not knowing what became of my soul? God sees.

"I have asked many doctors about the horrible reason, but I can swear to you, my brother that I shall not be asking them any-more, for I had twelve of them hanged, and eunuchized three, for their voice was too coarse and loud. And the one who told me that only after my death can the reason of the disease be judged, I had him buried alive in the graveyard, so that he conveniently cured corpses there. Then I asked people, aware of star paths and all the customs, very eerie, of sun and moon, these—having conferred long—answered me that only in one-hundred and seven years will appear in the sky the star with which my fate is connected. What should I do then?

"I had summoned all the sages that could be found in my coun-try, but two only arrived: one of them was dumb and therefore un-able to advise me anything; the other was a great wise man and very famous, but only in the game of chess, in which he exercised righ-teous fame, but he could not diagnose my disease. Therefore I bow down to your feet, grand and mighty sultan, and let my despair pros-trate with me, begging you for help. I know that nowhere on this earth can one find as many sages as there are in your immense country, and I know you are surrounded by their numerous circle, wisely soliciting you how to rule. Have one of them not to look for some time in your radiant face, and send him to my capital, to stand before me, and read from my eyes why the sea of sorrow swells across my soul, why there's a thorn in my heart, and my eyes are reddened with tears of blood. I am on fire!

"Greetings to you, mightiest of all the rulers, who if emerging at night, makes miracles; for birds start to sing and flowers blossom thinking that the day is dawning. You, without whom paradise is gloomy like my soul that you will see tonight in your dream, very pale and miserable, which you deign to forgive me, please, great and powerful Anianti, my brother."

This is a letter that proud Al Mahar was writing for many days and nights, then having taken a marvellous dagger, he gazed long in its bluish blade, and finally with one cut he slashed his arm, so that the signature reddened with blood. So little of it flew out though that it sufficed for three or four letters only, so exhausted with sorrow and grief was the noble Caliph that seeing it, worried gravely, but then having come up with a crafty idea, he called one cook of very sanguine complexion, and having swung his arm, he most graciously hit him between the eyes, so that the nose of the man flooded with blood. With it he finished the writing.

Then, great cavalcade set out for the seashore, and two tall men carried the Caliph's priceless letter in a sandalwood, gold encrusted chest, watching it carefully, more than their eyes, for it was easier for them to get new pair of eyes than for Al Mahar to write such a second letter that contained all his soul. One-hundred camels followed them in very opulent harnesses, and under the palanquins, so that the sun didn't swelter them too much and scorch their marvellous skin, rode one-hundred women, more beautiful than a most beautiful dream—when man rests full on his bed, his heart pure—all of them virgins that never knew a man, which having duly and craftily investigated the subject, confirmed the incorruptible eunuch overseer, an old hand in his job and hard to befool. Now riding on a tall and strangely mean dromedary, he pretended to be asleep, his eyes closed. Sometimes though, he would wake up suddenly and swish with his whip bare back of the slave, who, running alongside the camel, turned his eyes to look under a woman's palanquin, grinned and started to shiver like with a fever. And then would fall asleep again the virginal man, who shall never have a son, similar to himself.

Then followed many riches and numerous warfare tools, encrusted with gold, miraculously playing with the sunrays-all of this to regale the eye of Indian ruler. Further, in an endless train walked four strong men carrying a big board on which, with a red paint, was drawn a denouement of great geometrical problem, for Al Mahar wanted to show his noble brother how scholarly his subjects were; then followed the others, carrying all sorts of medicines for various illnesses, and another carrying a strange machine, emulating the hum of a storm and peal of the lightning; finally, three-hundred slaves trod slowly. Such plentiful treasures, so many virgins, and slaves offered Grand Caliph Al Mahar for one man that knew wisdom and beheld it with his own eyes.

He himself sat dolorous, and not speaking to anyone, he stared at the ceiling all day long; at night, he would lay on his back, and having ascertained that no one could overhear him, he groaned hollowly.

The Grand Vizier knew about it and Sheikh ul Islam knew about it; they knew it separately though, but whenever they met by accident, they would look at each other very sensibly; then the Vizier, in order not to say too much, would wink his left eye, and say with his right one: "It seems to me that our lordly Lord deigned to go mad!" and the Sheikh, having winked his right eye, would whisper with his left eye: "That's what happens when someone's stupid like a begging dervish." Then simultaneously, and fast, they would both squint their eyes, so that no trace was left of their conversation, and they would walk in opposite directions, seriously and very thoughtfully, and the Grand Vizier would think deeply and say to himself: "This thief, pretending devotion, fingers his prayer beads, for if his hands were free he would steal on every hand." And the Sheikh supposed in his soul that even a Grand Vizier, having stumbled on a stone, can break his leg. That's what they wished each other from the depth of their hearts, and Allah listened to both.

Al Mahar waited. There was no joy of life for him, for he couldn't find it anywhere, neither in the gardens, through which he maundered like a shadow, nor in the harem, where on silky cushions, sweetly dreaming, waited houris from all the corners of the earth, when he deigned to appear and choose one for pleasure—during which one sees heavens opened and a Prophet, sitting among the virgins—but Caliph hardly ever now walked through women's chambers and only in passing he deigned to look at some gorgeous breasts, brought forward with a movement of a fruit merchant showing the passersby two delicious pomegranates lying in his hand; he barely deigned to look at the rosy body of a houri that starkly exposed, sought to dazzle his tired eyes with splendour of shivering loins: that's how a Persian merchant wants to dazzle people's eyes, having spread before them a fine carpet, soft and fuzzy. Ooh!

Like birds twittering in the morning about night's adventures, so they, after the Caliph's passage, his footsteps strewn with flower petals and amber dust, were talking to one another, in a whisper as sweet as a myrrh scent and caressing like a sough of leaves in the gardens, when the evening breeze strokes them with its spidery palm: "Sad is our Lord, ruler of the half of the world, would that I could overjoy him tonight!" And another, her eyes quiet like a sigh, and skin as translucent as a candid heart, would say: "His body must be cold now, for sorrow torments him." Yet another, looking long where the black-haired Al Mahar disappeared, sighed only, thinking how miserable must he be, and started to cry, for she had only twelve years of age and plenty of tears uncried. A sloe-eyed eunuch noticed it, and being afraid that her eyes might redden, he enumerated her ten scourges with a thin bamboo stick, for her to hide her tears, and so it happened.

Al Mahar waited.

Many times had the moon sat on top of the highest minaret, like a golden bird that rests for a while, tired of a roam, but chased away with barking and howling of the dogs, detesting the sight of it, drifted down, slowly negotiating the stars, not to precipitate some tinier one of the firmament, as it sometimes happens, and then the star, having paled from deadly terror, shaken out of the great carpet of the sky plummets to the ground, dragging behind, spread in the wind, its long golden hair. The Caliph looked in the sky and counted moons, and whenever the moon died, devoured by greedy clouds like Mahar's soul by sorrow, the Caliph would rip one emerald out of his turban and throw it into the sea, not to lose count of time. Out of twenty four, only three emeralds were left on his fine turban, when it was reported that deputation of the Indian ruler heads for his palace and with them were none of the Caliph's people sent with gifts a long time ago

Al Mahar had new turban brought, inlaid with diamonds, finer than the one that the sun wears at dusk—immense purple calpack with the most beautiful jewels shining in a golden setting, embellished with a crest of feathery clouds, fluttering in the breeze. The proud crest on the Caliph's turban, spangled with diamond dust like with transparent dewdrops, was the one that Al Mahar rarely removed from the treasury, for he was told by one hodja (that later lost his mind) that Allah envies him it, not having suchlike, and it does not become to prick one's God's eyes with heron feather.

He then put on attire of marvellous colour, and on his shoulder a fine cloak, weighing with a thousand diamonds and the same number of rubies and slightly less emeralds and pearls, for so many jewels, oozing sun or blood, exuding verdancy or twinkling with mysterious seabed glow, were spangled throughout the fabric, shining like water surface at sunset, warm like a breeze in the desert and as soft as a woman's hand. So grand was Al Mahar in his outfit that his servants, having seen him, dropped to their faces and prostrated themselves, and one dervish, thinking that he would earn the Caliph's favour, pretended to rub his eyes, then, having dropped to his stomach, started to groan: "Prophet! Prophet!" Al Mahar wondered at first, and when the wonder left him, he ordered the dervish to stand up and most graciously, with his own hand, deigned to smack him on the slimy mug.

Then he took a breath and inquired, where the Grand Vizier was, and he was advised that the other was contemplating matters of great importance, the fate of the state depending on them. Caliph Al Mahar became worried about his servant and in all his brilliance, walked to Vizier's chambers himself, but having stood by the doors, he wondered for the second time, for the Vizier, sitting obliviously on a divan, was cracking walnuts with the great seal of state, as it was made of iron and very heavy. Great Al Mahar frowned and extinguishing his anger, said:

"Drop, what you are doing you son of a dog and come with me, to stand by my throne, when I receive a deputation and the greatest sage that ever walked the earth."

Like a dog, its tail drawn-in, follows its master, so the Vizier followed Al Mahar to the great hall, fountain springing up in the middle of it; fragrance wafted around it, weaving itself with barely perceptible mist, for plenty of scents were poured into the water, which was even advisable, as at this fountain, eunuchs and other court dignitaries washed their hands. It also happened that some, being too lazy and acting sloppily, poured what wasn't a rosy water at all, into the marble fountain's basin, which was, even without this, littered with all sorts of waste, dates, fruits, and even a sheep bone.

In the hall, sat on thirty nine cushions was dignified Caliph Al Mahar, and around sat dignitaries, showing great curiosity, which one could easily recognize on their faces, save for those that chewed delicacies or hard sheep veins and moved their jaws extensively; and the Caliph, his eyes lightly squinted, shone in riches and glamour of diamonds, like the splendid moon shines among the stars, and looked like a sleeping lion that having eaten to the full, now rests, buried in golden sand. He opened one eye though, having heard a clamor in the courtyard and the tramp of numerous sandals on its granite paving; and opened the other only when great rabble of weird men started to flock into the hall. They looked as sun burnt as a ram toasted on coals, and were so thin that even the thinnest dervish in the Caliph's state seemed to be, by comparison, fat like an unclean swine; it seemed that these people cast no shadow and that it is not them that are carrying long spears, but the spears are carrying them, waving them about, like wind waving a thin branchlet.

Their eyes were beautiful, and even darker than the soul of a great thief or the conscience of the Caliph's treasurer; these were the eyes big and judicious like the eyes of a camel, for the animal's sight is seven times more intelligent than the sight of a sage that knows by heart all suras of the Quran, and three-hundred and eleven times more intelligent than even the most crafty woman; their eyes seemed to comprehend everything and were devouring everything like a fire, so it was thing of a wonder that they were still so thin. Having seen them, Sheikh ul Islam thought that in the country of these odd people, one cannot use this exquisite and in many cases useful swearing: "Would that the flesh fell off your bones!", for one would have to be swearing for about three years on end, and there would not even be enough of fallen-off flesh to feed a crow. He was very anxious too, as was the Caliph, who opened his eyes wider and wider, astounded; as astounded would be the Prophet, seeing Ali Baba and his forty thieves suddenly enter the paradise.

And they first raised a horrible cry, so loud that the crest on the Caliph's turban swung suddenly, then they all dropped to their faces and were lying so for very long time, so that the Caliph could count them, and he counted up two-hundred men. Then one of them, apparently their commander, stood up, and the rest, kneeling, listened to his speech, shouting immensely every three words, which was supposed to advertise immense joy of their hearts. This is how their commander Muriamadasi spoke, his words stumbling on shiny teeth:

"Earth is great and Earth is greater, but you are the greatest, Sultan Al Mahar. There is many a wise and many a sage, but you are the wisest, Grand Caliph. These are not my words, but words of my master that said to me: 'Go to Caliph Al Mahar and tell him that he's the wisest, so that he'll be pleased in his heart, for so stupid is this man that he will believe in anything you wickedly tell him, O Muriamadasi.' This is what he said."

"Hoyo!" howled his comrades.

Al Mahar was reddened with horrible anger like a sun when its eyes redden with blood, so that the blood drips on the sea, and in a moment he paled like a man that having eaten excessively, is chok-ing and muddle-headed. Around him stood everybody, shivering of deadly fear, not daring to breathe, not to inhale with the air these disgraceful words, said out of sheer stupidity; the commander though, not considering the great impression given by his words, cherished carefully in his head during the long voyage, as if he cher-ished snake or a worm or a toad, continued:

"This is what my Master, who has a thousand elephants, ordered me to tell you: 'Greetings to you, my brother, Sultan of the faithful, who sent me one-hundred virgins as a comfort to my worries, but realize that out of the hundred only twenty-seven arrived at my country with virginal treasure; all the others were in quite different state, which I couldn't comprehend, and ask you for explanation, Caliph Al Mahar'."

"Hoyo!" roared the mob, bowing down at the sound of the frightful name.

"'Therefore (my Lord and ruler had me tell you this) I had all your people trampled by elephants, which should undoubtedly please you, for bad is a servant that doesn't respect his master's vir-gin. I wanted to send you many virgins too, Al Mahar, but my ser-vants looked for them for thirty days and nights in my entire coun-try and found only one, but she was lame, with lots of spots on her face. So I only send you two parrots and many diamonds, to distrib-ute it with scorn among your slaves. I also send you the one you de-manded: the man that seemed wise to me. Take him and do with him whatever you please, but I reckon it would be best if you have him killed, for he's too wise to be happy, and too wise to deserve life. Live long Caliph Al Mahar!' This was said by my Master, who has a thousand elephants, I said!"

"Hoyo!" shouted his comrades and banged their foreheads against the stone floor so hard that the granite slabs cracked in places, to everybody's greatest surprise.

Everybody wondered greatly and mused upon these words long, not rushing their thinking, to abstract properly all their sense; similarly a hungry man chews pumpkin stones, long and patiently, not to loose even a crumb of this noble fare, and like him, finally spitting out the remains, having extracted the gist of the speech, spat Caliph Al Mahar with just one word.

"Thief!" he whispered and started to muse.

Everybody gazed at him like at a rainbow, for he resembled one, waiting what he deigns to say; and he, after a long while, looked sternly at the deputation commander and loudly asked:

"Where is this man that claims to be wiser than the others?"

"This man is in the courtyard," answered the commander, "I ordered him to clean the camel, for being a sage he is not capable of doing anything more useful."

Al Mahar must have been very surprised, for he squinted his eyes and was speechless for a moment. Soon though, he looked wrathfully, then started to untie the green rope, serving him as a belt, and having thrown it under the feet of the Indian commander, said:

"Take this and do what becomes you."

Muriamadasi raised the rope from the ground and started to gaze at it with awe, not knowing what to do with such a splendid gift; his face swollen with amazement and interest, until he was approached by one mufti* that grabbed the rope, and having noosed it around the envoy's neck, clearly explained to him, what the Caliph's wish was.

"Hoyo!" groaned the servants of the Indian ruler, and Muriamadasi, having quickly understood how things were, prostrated thrice, then having kissed the rope with respect, withdrew on his knees to hang himself somewhere else to not strike the Caliph with a nasty view. And the Caliph, having breathed deeply, beheld all the gathered with horrible eye, then he adjusted himself on the cushions and sent the Vizier to the camel stables, where the Indian sage groomed a dromedary, labouriously scratching sun dried dung off its coat. The Vizier addressed him, his words noble and very deep:

"If you are the one that I'm looking for, come with me."

"I suppose I must be the one, if you have found me." answered the sage and having wiped his hands on his long beard, followed him humbly.

* * *

Caliph Al Mahar looked long and hard at the man from the far away country, considering how to recognize a sage, not knowing anything of his wisdom, but he couldn't find anything on the senile face that would be different from people of dense mind.

It was a man having more years than one can count out quickly, having inhaled thrice, his skull peeled of hair so neatly that even

---

* Islamic scholar

a locust peels the tree of its leaves with less care, or like a Caliph's treasurer, collecting taxes, peels poor people of their possessions; and no armour of fine damascene steel that sometimes shines like a sun (sometimes flashes with lurid blueness, as if blue blood clotted its golden veins), shone like the skull of this overseas sage; and no learned scribe in the Alexandrian library, no matter how strong, is able to polish so finely the donkey skin, on which later, like flowers, marvellous words shall blossom, like fate polished the skull of this man. His beard must have been white for a very long time; its hoariness streaked with yellow stripes, for even hoariness fades, and only Allah's beard of snowy, curly, southern clouds is eternally white.

Al Mahar looked in the sage's eyes and could not see anything in them, as one cannot glimpse a thing at the bottom of very deep well, where sleeps moist darkness and silence full of water. For a moment it seemed to the Caliph that a dark gleam out of the sage's eyes fell upon his pupils, as if a shadow, so that his soul darkened, and a sudden shiver ran down his spine, as happens in the desert when from red-hot sands suddenly blows cold, inconceivable dread, inhabiting under some dune or lurking in the carcass of a camel that died among the sands. Al Mahar looked as fast as he could at the old man's mouth and noticed on it a smile, as sweet as only oozes from a child's mouth. He marvelled as if he had seen a cadaver that smiles a lively smile; then he looked long and could see that the immense sweetness of it, not even for a moment leaves withered lips of an old man fused to them as flower fuses with the earth or heart with a heart, and is so devoted to the quiet face of a sage like a child to a mother, or friend to a friend, when they reconciled with each other and have sworn each other affection. Spake then Caliph:

"You were given eerie face by Allah, who acts eerily. Why are you smiling?"

"Why shouldn't I smile," answered the sage, "when I am looking at the sun?"

"Are you talking about me?"

"Great is your wisdom, O Caliph, for you comprehended my words instantaneously!" And smiled again the old man, a smile of a child that's only three years old and understands the language of birds, stones, and the sun, and the Caliph thought that the words of an old man are beautiful like houris and very meaningful, therefore he spoke favourably:

"You are a man of such sapience that you could be a Caliph."

"If I weren't a sage, I would like to be a Sultan."

"And who would you like to be if you were a Caliph?"

"I would like to be sapient man again."

These words seemed obscure to Al Mahar and he couldn't seize their meaning, as sometimes a warrior on a tired horse cannot seize the other, who on a fleeter horse than his own, escapes into the desert. So he gazed at the laughing face of a sage and this smile that wandered about his indifferent eyes, like a frivolous woman that having unclothed herself, circles the holy man, trying to seduce him to no effect. Then he said:

"I shall give you wonderful clothes and turbans made of silk; I shall give a sword too, for you to defend against a bad man." He had not even finished speaking when the sage laughed loudly, declaiming:

"Shall you give me women too?"

I shall give you ten, very beautiful, each without a mark on her body; all of them virgins."

"Why are you laughing?"

"Because I want to ask you to give me an eunuch."

"Why do you want him?"

"For he will be of more use to these beauteous houris than myself. Why do you want to harm them?"

Like a shot, Al Mahar understood what the old man meant to say, and pitied him in his heart, and to show him his favour, proclaimed him a prime judge in his country, for him to judge according to his great mind.

"You are acting amiss, Caliph," answered him the other, "for only a stupid and crafty man can tell good from bad, for being guilty himself, he shall uncover somebody else's guilt, knowing all the ways to cover a sin, as with a pile of withered leaves. What could I do though?"

"You shall judge, and Allah shall distinguish the truth."

"Don't you know that Allah is an old man that's not in a hurry? And what happens if I have an innocent hanged; will Allah cut him off the rope later?"

"Your word is bold, answered the Caliph, "and it becomes me not to listen to it. I hereby order you to commence the judgments, and when I behold your great reason, I shall call you and ask about great things that are out of this world. Now, leave in peace!

The sage bowed down to Al Mahar and left; and it seemed that wherever he walked, there becomes lighter and gloom quickly crawls into the corners, where the eye does not reach. Everybody wondered exceedingly, how come that such great splendour fell upon this ragamuffin, whose head was not inhabited by unclean vermin, only because he had no hair, and his decayed robe doesn't fall off him, for in some strange manner it holds on to his sticking-out bones. Spat behind him the slave that brought him food in a silver bowl; but the old man addressed him:

"If you love wisdom, take this fare and bring me two dates and small goblet of water, and I will tell no one that you ate my food." And when the slave brought him the modest fare, the sage asked him:

"Where is your father's home?" The slave beheld him fearfully, then said:

"On the Nile, my lord."

"You have lash wounds on your back;, do they hurt you a lot?"

"They have been stinging me for many days now."

"I shall tell you thus: Look at this blue sky and tell me, isn't your river as blue as the sky?"

The slave raised his head and long, long looked up; and whether of staring into the radiant celestial dome, or out of great pain, un-invited tears started to trickle down his swarthy cheeks, and he felt it only when they flowed into his mouth and settled onto his lips like a bitter aftertaste of poisonous herb; then he slowly detached his eyes from the firmament and through tears looked on the old man, who smiled like a child, and soon, born of salt of these tears, out of the gloomy and foggy eyes of the slave, a good and kind smile run down on his face.

"I have seen my river, my lord!" he whispered and having slipped to his knees, kissed thin hands of old man, and he, having stooped, spoke:

"Hide your pain deep in your chest, and paint your face with a smile; you shall suffer less and they will beat you less, for no one wants a servant with a gloomy sight. Respect your hatred and carry it deep, at the bottom of your heart—not on your lips, not to shout or sing it out too fast. You have nourished on this one smile for a long time. Go now, go!"

Saying it, he had sky on his face, light and laughing, as on a fine spring day. His eyes could not be seen, for he covered them with the eyelids, and so he remained in deep meditation, motionless like a monument made of yellow bone, as if he fell asleep or died with serenity on his face, which happens to people knowing death not only by name, but also by the face, so not terrified by it. When the death comes for such a man, it bows deeply to his knees and says: "Let us go!" And he asks: "Is this far?" "Even further." answers him death. "Be welcomed in my home as a sister that came to visit her brother! Just let me, o death, smile.". Blenches the death, because for a smile, one has to await sometimes even a hundred years or sometimes even longer, so it looks him in the eyes, long and inquiringly, weighing its thoughts, then says: "I can see your soul, and at its very bottom there is a smile, therefore retrieve it from the depths, like a pearl diver from the water abyss, and die." Then dies this man, like a kid dreaming of flowers and blue birds, or its mother's heart.

Like this dead man looked the sage at the moment, his face throwing a golden reflection on the great misery of his body and garment, so that he was gilded all over and as if elevated over the ground. In such a condition, he was found by a Grand Vizier, who came in the Caliph's name, to summon the sage for trial. He stooped over the sage and before he touched his arm, he pondered silently: "Can this camel's tail be a sage that is supposed to try the dignitaries? What will happen is that a malefactor that stole a mule, who is about to be tried by him, will spit in his face and ask to be hanged without a trial, just not to hear the sentence from the mouth of this dead jackal. The Caliph lost his mind long ago, now it seems he has lost his eyes too, or maybe they have been stolen from him by the Sheikh, who steals everything that shines... I also wonder," thought the Vizier smiling with contentment, "what would you do to me, if you had power over me, you swine?"

"I would have you hanged!" the sage said suddenly, his eyes opened a moment earlier, answering the question that only Allah could hear (for it was a fine day and there was no din in the world), but even he could not hear it, for it was not said with words, but expressed within great secrecy of thought.

The Grand Vizier reeled, like a suddenly wounded beast, and paled as much as a timid woman, whose womb has suddenly been exposed; his eyes goggled, and mouth opened so widely that one could see two teeth of green colour, not as marvellous as two emeralds, but because of their deserted solitude, dignified. He froze in his wince and lasted so long, before one green tooth hit the other in a failed attempt to jingle, that one could only hear wheezing out of his throat, as often among the moonlit silence of a desert produces a mangy jackal choking on the bone of dead horse. Only after a while, one word, pulling the other by the turban out of the abyss, made it to his lips.

"What... do you know... about me?"

The old man smiled.

"Mercy me!" groaned the Vizier, "You hear a rustle of thoughts and you are the wisest among the mankind. Oo! Oo! But I thought thus on purpose," he added craftily, "wanting to see whether you really, as I have heard, read thoughts and see inside the heart; look deeper though and you will see that I hold you in great respect and I am able to offer ten uncut coins for you to see how much I love you."

"Grand Vizier," answered the sage, "I haven't seen your thoughts, I have seen your eyes, for you think with your eyes. Tell me now, what's the purpose of your visit?"

"The Caliph calls you to judge an important case; if that be your will, raise your noble body and have it proceed to the courtyard, where my lord is smoking hookah and ruminating deeply. I must warn you though that he is angry, and his eyes fling lightnings, for an hour ago he had his cook slaughtered, having found in the tasty dish, a piece of old yellow turban, which colour the sultan detests the most. Follow me, Sir!"

This said, he bowed humbly and went forward, and the old man stepped behind him, carrying the smile on his face, like an emaciated slave that brings his worried master good news. He saw sitting the Caliph, his head stooped. Over him, the servant was waving a giant fan of ostrich feather, driving off the sun and the flies; around him stood many dignitaries, overbearing and very dour, their turbans sporting diamonds or other invaluable jewels, as if they smashed the sun to pieces with a hammer and each took one sunny part. They all pouted with great contempt, looking at the new favourite that has just approached his master's person, without fear on his face and failing to greet him with a bow, said:

"Here's your judge, Caliph; now, have the malefactors step forward from your entourage."

Hearing these words, so rude, some reached for their daggers, one started to jerk his black beard, like a village woman hackling flax, many though looked at the Caliph with fear, their faces paled. The Caliph liked these words though, for he released a great cloud of smoke out of his mouth, and with a smoke he mixed these words:

"You shall try, in my presence, five women, who were in the harem of my servant Hassan.

"Why did not he try them himself, if they had done something wrong?"

"Because he hanged himself out of desperation; even though he died, I had him punished with hundred lashes, for he hadn't paid the taxes, which he should have done before his death."

"What did his wives do then?"

"The five wives of Hassan shamefully surrendered their bodies to another man, which can be confirmed by venerable Abd ul Moshed, who did not turn up though, for he went down with a strange disease: he locked himself in the stable with his donkey and speaks only to it, from time to time jerking the beard out of his face, touched with some immense despair. Did you understand the case?"

"Hassan could not understand it and therefore he hanged himself, but as these were not my wives, I can understand the case, and try it willingly. Where are these doves, Caliph?"

Al Mahar motioned and not much time passed, when before the gathering, were stood five women, each accompanied by two very tall servants; their faces were veiled, only the eyes visible, very red, undoubtedly of tears, although a woman crying, can cry with her whole body, with her hands, bosom, and head, but very rarely with her eyes, just for them not to redden afterwards.

Sat before them the noble sage and measured them with his eyes, which they were doing too, wondering very much, how can he be a judge, a man looking so kindly and with such soft, sunny smile on his face; they were even more surprised, having heard his kind voice, as if flowing straight from his heart, full of scent and balm. Spake the old man:

"It is all the same, by what name the woman goes, therefore I am not asking what your names are, nor will I tell you that you must die according to law, for you probably are well aware of that. If such be the grace of grandest Sultan, then he might think: 'treacherous woman died, although she is still alive, so there's no need to punish her with death.' He may also think like this, in his great soul: 'If from beginning of the world, there existed a death penalty for an unfaithful woman, would there be even one left as a solace of my days?' And if his clemency is immeasurable, then he will think for the third time: 'What do I care about a mangy sheep or such woman that committed adultery?'"

Great Al Mahar remained silent, listening with interest to the words of a judge, and did not mind them. He thought that it was how he should have been thinking, and if he did not that was only because of excessive heat, for the sun went mad on that day; so he listened on in silence, like his entourage, and the sage, polishing his every word with a smile, continued:

"Only a jackal or other unclean creature can converse with a treacherous woman; therefore the grandest Caliph chose me for this function, so that neither him nor anyone from his nobles became defiled, asking you about your guilt; and after the trial they shall rinse their eyes with water, for they looked at you too long. Therefore I am telling you: None of you will die in a harem and be buried under a cypress, as it is done to a matron that protected her purity. He who tries you, is acting amiss, for it is wasting one's time in vain that could be dedicated to musings or other sensible things. But a righteous judge should do everything to tear the malefactor out of the hands of the law, as from the mouth of a lion, for he is not a judge to rush suspects to death with a leather whip, but to take the victim away from the death. Law is made of stone and of stone is its heart, so this man should be of kind heart, and having dropped to the feet of the great pyramid of law, should beg that eternally asleep, opened its eyes for a moment and beheld. He, who looks with nimble eyes, will see a lot." This said, he turned to the Caliph and bowing down his head he said:

"These women are fated for death, aren't they, O Great Al Mahar?"

"You said! spake the Caliph. The sage weighed some thought long, then said:

"You ordered me to be a judge, and now, kindly, let me be it. I will ask each of these women, in turn, why they committed adultery, and you promise me, to let go the one that gives the real reason."

"How can you tell which one is telling the truth?"

"I shall ask my years, and if they cannot tell, I shall ask my brains; and if my brains cannot tell it either, then I shall ask my soul that is older than me and my brains and remembers the birth of the moon and the moment when in the firmament there were only two stars that then propagated into great starkind. Do me this favour Caliph, and thus content my heart."

Al Mahar glanced at everyone and saw faces marked with patronizing smiles and hilarity in everyone's eyes; thus realizing, he could easily allow it, for none of the five will tell the truth, and they all be met with righteous and exemplary punishment. So he said:

"I can promise you this!"

At this moment, the five women winced, their bosoms started to heave, and eyes shoot in all directions, as if looking for help or escape; one could also see that their legs shivered and knees wobbled; like those of a camel that, tired of a long way, longs to drop to its knees, but for the great fear of beating, keeps straightening its legs. The old man beheld them compassionately, then spoke:

"It always happens that if a woman tells the truth, she dies, being unable to survive this horrible moment. Today though, the one telling the truth shall survive, as it should be, because with the truth, one can protect oneself even from Allah's anger, and a lie is like shield made of goat skin, which will not withstand the cut of a sword nor will it protect the heart. Tell me then, you, who are lofty as minaret spire, why it happened that you had offered your body, belonging to your husband Hassan, who hanged himself, to someone else, as if it were a rotten date, not a body?"

The woman, to whom these wise words were addressed, faltered abruptly, and dropping to her knees, started to groan heavily, then, having jerked a wisp of hair out of her head, spoke:

"I had been starved by this man, so that I was helpless when some stranger attacked and took me when I felt faint. This is the truth and nothing but the truth, righteous judge."

As sun, sometimes eclipsed with a cloud, or dusk appearing on the earth out of nowhere, so the face of old man darkened, and the smile dropped off it like a golden curtain.

"Your truth is ridiculous," he said "And your body proves your words are a lie. Take her!"

Two dreadful servants grabbed the woman, although she raised a shout, as fierce as even does not shout a cobbler, from whom silk shoes were stolen; very little time passed before they had sewn her into a leather sack and tied a stone to it, then having swung strongly, flung her into the water that splashed, terrified. The second woman spoke:

"On previous days Hassan has beaten me with a strap, so I have done it out of vengeance."

The sage mused.

"Woman," he said, "avenging herself, will do even the most mindless thing; it can be that she shall chop her own leg off with an axe, or rub pepper in her eyes so that her husband that paid a lot for her, suffered severe harm. Tell me though, having committed the betrayal, have you told Hassan about it, for him to grieve?"

"No." she answered, "I was afraid that he would beat me again."

"How did you avenge yourself then, him not knowing anything about it?"

"My grudge was not that strong, for him to learn..."

"Take her!" the sage answered to it, and lowered his head on his chest, not wanting to see as the second woman is being sewn into the sack to throw her and her truth into the water. A long moment then passed before the old man, with his eyes, asked the third woman, who started to speak fast, as if she'd prepared her words beforehand and threaded them onto the memory cord like amber beads or like one threads figs onto a flexible branchlet; one word chasing the other, like a dog chasing a deer, all of them winded, and oozing tears like sweat of weariness.

"My Lord," she spoke "I swear to Allah that I resisted long, but I couldn't resist him when he brought me a diamond necklace and so many great pearls that I could not tot them up for three days and three nights."

Everybody cocked their ears, even the Caliph himself glanced at her slightly; but the sage looked at her pitifully, then asked:

"Is he a prince, or a Caliph's brother, or maybe Ali Baba, possessing the biggest treasures of all?"

"I wouldn't have slept with a thug. It's an honest man."

"Don't you know what his trade is?"

"I know well that this man, the reason of my misfortune, sells goats milk to pilgrims passing by the city."

"For how long have you been counting the pearls then?"

"For three days and three nights. Why, I have told you this before, my Lord."

"Take her!" said the sage and with a flap of his robe, wiped the sweat off his dark-amber forehead, then having taken a breath, raised his eyes to the sky and was slightly moving his lips, like a man that prays silently. The sun fell straight on his face, so he squinted his eyes slowly, and speaking no more, motioned the fourth woman to speak. That one spoke with voice trembling and quiet:

"I have done a very bad thing, for I very much loved Hassan, my husband. I took into my head to get to know the other man, so that when immensely kind Hassan, would come to me, I could tell him: 'I have thought that the other would be better, but you are above the all!' I expected he would gladly hear such words and be proud that for me he was the one and only"

"Take her!" said the sage, louder than before and shivered, hearing her immense lament and grumble; then he shivered again, having heard a silent laugh of many dignitaries, who were already tired of the scenes, their ears full of screams and cries of these deceitful women, for whom it would have been better if they weren't born at all.

The Caliph hasn't moved though, so they waited patiently, in depth of their souls pitying the unfortunate judge that looked for the truth in a woman, and they thought to themselves that he's like a fool looking for water in the middle of the desert, or a diamond in a puddle, or stroking the serpent's back, addressing it with erudite words. They silenced their whispers though, seeing old man rising scarcely and approaching the last woman, trembling slightly; her head lowered on her chest, eyes covered with lids, and so she stood quietly, without a cry. He told her:

"At the bottom of deep water, your sisters are looking for the truth now, having noticed too late that the truth dwells this deep. Have you heard them cry?"

The woman didn't say a word.

"Allah won't hear their cry now and nor can a Prophet's eye see them; but there is still one more leather sack, for which it would be better if it carried donkey's milk or water from a tank, than be sewn up with you inside. Will you tell the truth, wife of Hassan?

The woman pursed her mouth and didn't answer.

"Oh!" sighed the wise, old man. "It is bad when a woman speaks, but it is even worse when she remains silent. And let me tell you this: One who speaks a lot, tells less lies; the one that doesn't say a word, tells a hundredfold lies. Thus, one is deceiving oneself, and oneself cannot trust. Why aren't you answering me?

She breathed deeper, but said nothing.

"The Caliph is growing impatient, and rough water that long be-came still can easily be disturbed again; I am afraid that the Caliph might motion these, who with strong arms can effortlessly lift and fling you far offshore. Will you tell the truth? Why did you give yourself to a man, whose name was not Hassan, who neither was similar to him, nor bought you, nor knew your father, to get you as a gift?

The woman didn't say a word. Then the old man dropped his hands, like a lumberjack that having long wrestled the tree, rooted deeply into the ground, failed to budge it, or like a man whose donkey, standing on a bridge, refuses to step forward, although its master, his legs dug in the ground, is pulling its harness, all out. Although, as if he wanted to save her at any price, he motioned his servant and ordered him to stretch the woman on the ground and unclothe this part of her body, which as of then no one had seen before, save for Hassan and this unknown man that traded goat milk.

Seeing what happened, everybody shouted in great voice, and the Caliph asked sternly:

"What do you want to do?"

"I will have her scourged, so that she would speak. Murmur rose, and Sheikh ul Islam, a man immensely proficient in these matters, said in loud voice:

"Realize, old man that this is banned, and a woman cannot be unclad by a male stranger!"

"My lord," answered the sage, "I know that the face shouldn't be unveiled, for that's what the Quran says, but have a look. Is this a face, the thing I uncovered?"

"Eh?" marvelled the Sheikh. And the Caliph, at whom everyone looked awaiting his words, said after much thought:

"Indeed, this thing bears little resemblance to a face."

Sudden murmur admired the great Caliph's wisdom and everybody started to flock, to see at close quarters, this sight, rare and beautiful; their eyes goggled, some faces as if in ecstasy; some didn't dare to breathe, as if anxious not to scare the view away; another thought he was in a desert that lures the traveller into doom with celestial images; and one very aged pasha opened widely his mouth, saliva trickling down his beard out of his foul snout.

The sage motioned with his thin hand, and a bamboo stick swooped down like a lightning held with the dexterous hand of a servant who was so terrified, as if he wasn't the beating, but the beaten one, and oblivious out of fear, he beat violently and long, until everybody's mouths widened in greasy, slimy smile.

"Go away!" cried out the old man eventually, and wanted to heave her off the ground, but his powers didn't last him; so she toiled up herself, but being unable to stand up, she just kneeled, wobbling. The sage took her hands and with a voice as kind as a mother speaks to a child, he asked:

"Will you answer?"

"Yes!" she whispered.

"Will you tell the truth that you can swear to Allah?"

"I will."

"Silence!" shouted someone from the noble bevy, "The Caliph wants to hear.

And foreign sage asked her with strangely soft voice:

"Answer me, why did you give yourself to a stranger?" She panted heavily for a while, then spake:

"I swear to Allah, to my mother and my father, I don't know why I have done it."

"What does she say?" asked the Caliph, surprised.

"She says, she doesn't know why she did it, my Lord."

Everybody looked at the sage, whose face was embellished with a sunny smile again; he raised his hands up in the air and said in stentorian voice:

"Say it again, woman."

"I don't know, my Lord, why I betrayed my husband, Hassan. Have me killed."

At this moment the sage turned to the Caliph and said, great silence surrounding him:

"Here, this woman, Grandest Sultan, told the truth and she shall live, as you promised.

"I see that you are delighted." said the Caliph, "Why should you care?"

"I am not delighted with her, my Lord," answered the old man, "But with finding my truth in her truth, now I know that a woman can do many things and commit horrible deeds, but she never knows why she is doing it."

"Let her go in peace." said the Caliph in the midst of great silence, for the amazement rendered everybody speechless. Al Mahar pondered upon something for a very long time, which could be seen on his forehead that wrinkled like a sea before it explodes with a tempest, prepared somewhere at the bottom of its abysmal chest; one could only hear soft rustle of ostrich feathers, which with great richness fluttered over the pensive Caliph's head, and the fast breathing of the sage, who seemed very tired. The Caliph, leaning towards him, said:

"I have understood her answer, and see clearly she has told the truth. I can also see that you comprehend more than the others and you know the paths not beaten by anyone. Tomorrow, when the day is done, and the night reaches the roof of my palace, come to me, and you shall hear what I only know. Do you know what you are going to see, tomorrow night?"

"I do not know, Grandest Sultan."

"Tomorrow, in starlight, you shall see the soul of Caliph Al Mahar."

It is a thing of wonder, how many things in this world are similar to a camel, but it is not similar to any of those; for even this coming night, despite having a thousand and one shapes, its most distinct form is that of a camel, maybe because it blows from the desert. Like this noble animal, its nostrils widened runs with great steps, the wind quickly like a snake crawling before him, so the night, having moved from the sandy dunes, runs heaving two vast hunches of clouds on its back and a grand, adorned with stars palanquin of the sky, made of black silk. The human eye cannot see who is sitting in its shadow, but it would be strange, if it weren't the grandest houri, smelling the smell of cyclamen, the one that makes sweet idleness of a paradise pleasant to the Prophet and whom he visits most often.

One can see from afar, how the huge camel of the night dashes ahead, sometimes causing the palm tops to flutter from the excessive scud, and sometimes a light to be blown out suddenly by the wind. Long ago has the muezzin chanted up his prayers, sweet as a memory of paradise, then looked long, his eyes filled with tears of emotion, to where left the sun, the pious pilgrim that with his elucidated and joyful face, hurries from Mecca to Medina. At last, the face of the night darkened completely and halting its rush, started to creep close to the ground, so that one could hear and feel its hot breath, like a breath of a woman in time of great bliss, slower and slower, and finally great silence, imbued with darkness throughout, started to squeeze in, like waters of the deluge, through every chink, first to homes, then to people's chests. It finally happened that even the greatest felon, drunk with silence, like with hashish, fell asleep on his bed, and a knife slipped from his hand.

At this hour, the foreign sage silently entered the chamber, in which sat the Caliph with his head bowed down, and said:

"You wanted to see me, Al Mahar!"

"You said," whispered the Caliph, "but I would rather listen to you."

"Isn't it better to listen to the night that is wise?"

The Caliph mused. "No." he answered after a while. "for night doesn't heal, but kills. Sit before me."

The sage did as he was told and waited in great respect, what the noble ruler, beheld by the sun when he rode on a white steed, and admired throughout the world, will tell him. Caliph remained silent for very long time though, maybe because he weighed some great thought in his heart, like a warrior that first weighs the spear in his hand before the throw, to hit the target with greater precision, or maybe he searched for beautiful and priceless words in his head, like a rich man searches diamonds and amethysts in his bag, in order to dazzle a pauper. Finally he spoke neither wisely nor beautifully, but strangely.

"Foreigner," he said, "I'm very unhappy." The other answered:

"Have more lamps lit, and you shall not see your misfortune, so visible in the dark. What does your misfortune look like, Caliph?

"It has green eyes, like a panther and is black like one; I can see it clearly when my eyes are open and even better when my eyes are closed. Isn't my misfortune astonishing?"

"You are astonished by it, therefore it is astonishing; in fact your misfortune is laughable, Al Mahar."

"What did you say?"

"Your misfortune is as small as grain of sand."

"You are not at all weighing words you throw into the darkness, old man. How can it be small, the misfortune of a Caliph? Is a Caliph a coffee merchant or a dervish?

"You said it, not me. Even less though weighs the Caliph, who is miserable, for there is no one to send a green rope for him to hang himself."

One could not recognize at night, whether the lamp flickered lighter, or the caliph paled, it was visible though that his hand grabbed a dagger with a rapid movement. The old man noticed it, but without even moving a muscle, said:

"I have been looking for death for so many years that I have forgotten their number. Why are you trying to frighten me with it, Al Mahar? Only a bad and stupid man is frightened of death, or a child or a woman; therefore if you want to scare me with it, I shall think that you are scared of it yourself. Did you call me to see it?"

The Caliph was breathing very fast, for his anger propelled his lungs, like a hasty blacksmith pulling the billows too forcefully, not considering that too much blood flows into his heart due to excessive heat. So heated were the Caliph's words, when he spoke:

"You defy my hands that are fast. Why are you doing this? Listen, old man: I know you have wisdom that only the few possess, I therefore want to talk to you favourably, and you, having listened to me, tell me what to do, so that the joy flows into my heart together with blood. Realize though that many listened to me before, but none of them is alive now.

"You pay like a Caliph." interrupted the sage.

"I reward like a Caliph too. Why are you smiling?"

"Haven't you seen me smile even in the daytime?"

"I have seen it and thought to myself: Wisdom gives buoyancy and buoyancy gives happiness. You must be very happy having perpetual smile on your face. Am I right in thinking so?"

The sage said nothing, he only looked on Al Mahar with his strange eyes and smiled so movingly that it seemed to the Caliph's imagination, aflame with night that the dead man laughed.

"Who are you?" he asked.

"I don't know yet." answered the old man. "If I die before you do, I will come to you at night and tell you, Caliph Al Mahar." He said it with a very sad voice, similar rather to singing than to a regular speech.

"You speak obscurely, as becomes the sage."

"The night is to blame that my words seem obscure, or maybe you do not hear them clearly, for they are very quiet. You can see my smile though?"

"I can see. I do not know though, where is the smile born that never dies?"

"In pain."

"What did you say?"

"It is born in pain and suffering."

"If this was the case," said the Caliph, "I would have it on my face, for I suffer immensely. My pain comes from the heart and soul."

"Your pain comes from stomach and liver."

"Bismillah!" groaned Al Mahar surprised.

"What have you suffered, Caliph?

"Bismillah!" repeated Al Mahar, "Your talk is the howling of a dog, if you ask me such question. Realize, you fool that in my entire country there is no man that would suffer as much as I did, and so big is my country that one needs four-hundred sixty and three days to ride round it on a fleet camel. I have been suffering for many days. I no longer know what joy or smile is; I have been suffering a pain in my soul for many moons now, which can be testified by anyone, for everybody sees that my face is sorrowful and all the pleasure has left me. You are not seeing this, for your eyes are old, and sorrow neither shines nor twinkles for even a blind man to see, but it is like grey ashes where a bonfire used to be. Do you comprehend?"

"You don't comprehend yourself, so how could I comprehend you, Caliph? When has your suffering started?"

"I don't know." answered Al Mahar. "It came out of nowhere and I don't know when."

"Have you pondered before, matters so deep that at the very thought of it, one suffers vertigo, as if looking in the abyss?"

"I was always afraid to think of such things, for they make me nauseous and grip my throat; therefore I ordered the Grand Vizier to muse upon them."

"You've done the right thing, Al Mahar. Tell me though, haven't you ever mused if there are wretches among your subjects?"

"It cannot be, when I'm the Caliph. Therefore I didn't bother my thought with it."

"What were you thinking about then?"

"Can you stop waves in the sea, to memorize their shape? How do you want me to remember what I thought about long ago?"

The sage thought for a while, then said:

"You shut all the doors before me, so that I cannot enter the palace of your soul and spot the evil-doer that hid in your chest and cuts your heart with a blunt knife. Show me your soul, Al. Mahar, and tell me all about it."

"My soul is very unhappy."

"Oooh!" said the sage, "Don't you know anything more about it"

"Forsooth, I don't know anything more."

"And you want me to heal it?"

"You said!"

"Do you want anything more?"

"I want you to teach me your smile. What do you want for it?"

Like a merchant displaying his most precious ware, smiled the sage with this silent, good smile, similar to a flower scent and twitter of a bird, to a whisper of palm trees and song of houris, and Al Mahar stared at the smile with a predatory look, as if he wanted to rip it off the old man's face.

"If you want to buy my smile," spoke the sage, "then tell me Caliph, how you can pay for it?"

The Caliph spoke speedily:

"In my treasury there are so many precious stones that even thirty slaves cannot upheave them. Do you want them?"

"It's not enough!" said the sage and smiled.

"I have six thousand dromedaries and three thousand camels carrying two hunches; I have six thousand horses and three thousand mares, and countless donkeys and mules."

"It's not enough!" said the sage.

"I have one thousand and two hundred wives, and I won't keep even one. Do you want them?"

"It's not enough!" carried on the sage, as if he had forgotten all the other words out of senility, and the Caliph panting quickly, enumerated:

"I will give you all the slaves I have in my lands."

"It's not enough!"

"I shall give you a ring with wisp of the Prophet's hair in it."

"It's not enough!"

"Allah! groaned the Caliph, "I will give you the green cloak of the Prophet and have your grave worshipped."

"It's not enough; still not enough!"

"I shall give you my turban and my sword, my sceptre, and my name. Do you want to be a Caliph?"

"All this is not enough!" answered the sage and laughed, his sight immensely compassionate.

And the Caliph weakened and reclined on the cushions like a very ill man, and squinted his eyes out of excessive effort. Many a step the night made, its eyes fixed on the east, before he spoke:

"It is immense luck that nobody heard my words, for the news would spread throughout my country that Caliph Al Mahar went mad; but you are the one that is mad. I thought you should be worshipped, but you are only entertaining me, you fool. I will tell everybody: I couldn't sleep, so I called a jester to make me laugh."

"No one is going to believe you, Al Mahar."

"Why not?"

"Because there is no smile on your face."

"Kesim!"* groaned the Caliph and stared at the old man with sight so horrific that many a slave would drop dead blazed with his master's eyes; but the old man looked at him as one looks at the child that does not know the reason of its mood, and remained silent. Finally Al Mahar, catching his breath with difficulty, said:

---

* beheading, slaughter.

"If you are not a madman, tell me, what do you want for the smile?"

"Two blood drops from your heart." answered the old man slowly and audibly, in such a manner though that sudden cold flew across the chamber, and sent shudders down Al Mahar's spine.

They both stopped breathing, and in great silence one could hear all the rustles of the night, similar to those of sand pouring in an hourglass or a quiet sobbing; and sometimes it seemed that in rhythmic intervals, a great hot tear trickled down the face of the night and dropped on the stones. And the Caliph felt cold in his heart, spreading throughout his body, for when he raised his hand to his forehead, he perceived how cold it was. It also happened that his thoughts became cold and sneering like steel blade from Toledo, whose shine is derisive and deathlike, and is cold as ice, so that it could not hesitate, searching a human's heart. The sage continued:

"Your heart has not so far spilled a blood drop, even as little as a dewdrop on a leaf, for it is faint and lazy. Why do you deceive me, saying your life is suffering? You are extremely bored, Caliph Al Mahar, but you reckon that this is your heart in tatters. Why do you blaspheme against your heart? East and West belong to Allah, but your heart belongs to you, but still you despised it. Why are you groaning? Do you think I will teach you art of smile, greatest of the earthly arts, which even the Prophet didn't master, for he didn't see his work in all its glory? I will tell you this only: one has to live a hundred years in this world and wriggle with pain as a bug thrown into the fire, before one day, you say to yourself 'I understand it now!' Then you shall smile, and the smile will never leave your face."

"Why do you demand just two blood drops from me?"

"Sometimes even one drop, spilled in inhumane pain, weighs more than a hundred years of suffering and sometimes with the great grace of Allah, one can comprehend in a blink of an eye, more than in a century. O, how lucky is this man who can buy so cheaply the knowledge of good and evil!"

"Have you ever been this happy?"

"Why do you want to see my heart, which is hidden very deeply?"

"In your chest?"

"No, in my grave. Why, Al Mahar?"

"Carry on," said the Caliph, "The night is drawing to a close."

"If you let me speak, I will tell you: Does a man that is drowning in the sea, overrun by the waves smile; don't you feel the wave roaring above you, Al Mahar? You are petty and unable to lift yourself up, therefore petty things and matters flooded you, and instead of looking at them from a distance, you are unable to get out of the swamp, for everything burdens you and pulls you down. If you want to heal your soul, drop it all, and not telling anyone, with staff in your hand, go out in the desert at dusk, and tell everyone you meet on your way: 'Haven't you heard that tonight has died Caliph Al Mahar, who thought he was very unhappy?' And in the desert, look long and hard, your eyes fixed on a traveller's path, where pass leprosy and smallpox, despair and poverty, hunger and thirst, and in your thought, seek for the great reason. Act so for many days, until you feel that all things earthly are minor and everything passes; that all has its limit and its bounds and that all your affairs are worth less than a camel's dung, which can be thrown into the fire. Great shall be the pain of your heart, before you tear yourself away from the things that you loved so much and before you comprehend that it is all trifle compared to the great mystery, from which escapes a man that is lazy, mean, and stupid, just as you did escape. And when you comprehend that you are dust and value less than a sigh, you shall say to yourself: 'I knew Al Mahar that used to be Caliph, but today he is very miserable!' You shall feel that your heart is squeezed in a sudden pain and remains so, and then you shall see nothingness, nothingness, and nothing but nothingness. Then you shall smile, and your smile shall be wise and it shall wisely expound you on everything; you won't hate anyone, and will renounce everything."

The Caliph listened, frowned his forehead, hatred in his eyes and great anger; he considered the words of an old man and they seemed to him like an insubordinate servant, who neither bows down before his master, nor respects his splendour and majesty. And whenever he looked at the sage's face, seeing the smile blooming in its kindness, he winced. "Do you understand everything?" he asked.

"I understand you, Caliph."

"He who understands all, will find the reason of it all and forgive everything?"

"You said, Al Mahar. I am pleased with your words."

"And you will forgive me, whatever I do to you?"

"You rightly said."

"Oh!" sighed the Caliph, "You are saying then that for two blood drops from my heart I shall learn your smile that comprehends and renounces everything? And you are also saying that your smile was born of great suffering and pain?"

"You said, my Lord!"

"Do you realize you've offended the Caliph, doubting his enormous pain?"

The old man smiled. Dawn was coming up already, for sudden cold was covering with hoarfrost their every word, so that they look nobly; in the courtyard one could already hear the neighing of the horses and the squeal of fighting camels. The Caliph raised slowly, not looking at the sage, clapped his hands, and when before him knelt a dour sentry, black as a saitan, he told him:

"Take this man and have his head cut off in the courtyard." And he beheld maliciously the sage, whose smile was now similar to the sunray.

"Faster!" shouted the Caliph.

"May peace be upon you, Al Mahar!" said the latter and followed the servant slowly, then having turned back from the door again, he uttered these words:

"Remember that joy of life lies in suffering."

"Begone! said the Caliph and sat heavily, waiting.

A long moment passed before one dignitary came and having prostrated, waited in silence to be questioned. The Caliph, not looking at him, asked:

"What do you want?"

"I came to tell you, Grandest Sultan that this man's head is off." The Caliph remained silent, and the other, unasked, spoke:

"The slave that had been told to cut his head off, didn't want to do it, then crying, he flung himself on his own blade and died. I beheaded the old man myself."

"Did he say anything?"

"He was only smiling, without a word, but there's a strange thing."

"Speak!"

"When his head rolled on the stones, the smile disappeared."

"Does this surprise you, fool?"

"Not this, Grand Caliph! But when they raised the head, it was as if its eyes came back to life and out of his pupils flowed tears of blood. He was a false sage, and only pretended to laugh. O, Allah! The head is still crying!"

This heard, the Caliph reached for his dagger, but he hadn't the strength to kill him, for having reeled madly he swooned. No one watched the face of the Lord that day, and at night disappeared the Grandest Caliph and no one could figure out what became of him. The Grand Vizier whispered to the Sheikh with wink of his left eye:

"Weren't I rightly saying that Caliph Al Mahar had long gone mad?"

"You said!" answered the Sheikh with his right eye.

Liked the book? Possibly hated it? Have your say:
http://forum.zalte.com